PRAISE FOR 52 STEPS TO RADICAL SUCCESS

"Angie provides a comprehensive guide to strategic decision-making and effective leadership in today's fast-paced corporate environment. *52 Steps to RADical Success: A Year of Breakthrough Strategies for Business and Life*, is packed with practical insights and actionable strategies. This book is a valuable resource for aspiring entrepreneurs and seasoned business professionals alike."

Tim Rail, Principle, CMR Alliance

I have had the privilege of working with Angie for the past decade. She has been instrumental in guiding and transforming my approach to business strategy, leadership, and personal development. Her impact on my professional journey has been profound, and by reading this book, you can start your journey to RADical success!

Torri Schaffer, Torri's Legal Services

"I've known and worked with Angie for many years. She always has amazing insight into the situations my business is facing and provides clear, succinct, no-nonsense guidance on getting past the challenge. These 52 strategies are the RADical blueprint to keep your business on track for success. This book should be on every business owner's 'Must Read' list!"

Scott Samborn, Principle, Aspen Management

Angie helps people to get things done! *52 Steps to RADical Success* offers practical tips and actionable plans for recognizing your potential and achieving your goals. She has created a brilliant, easy to use, no-nonsense resource. TAKE ACTION NOW and buy this book.

Sherry McCool, McCool Consulting

52 STEPS TO RADICAL SUCCESS:

A YEAR OF BREAKTHROUGH STRATEGIES FOR BUSINESS AND LIFE

ANGIE DOBRANSKY

52 Steps to RADical Success A Year of Breakthrough Strategies for Business and Life

Some of these chapters previously appeared in different form on the blog RADStrategic.com

Publisher Information
BelieversBookServices
4356 Montebello Dr
Colorado Springs, CO 80936

For more information, to purchase books in bulk, or to contact the author, please email angiedobransky@RADStrategic.com
ISBN 978-1-7361237-5-1 (softcover)
ISBN 978-1-7361237-6-8 (eBook)
Library of Congress Control Number: 2024914911

Cover design: John Quade
Editorial Team: Dr. Mark Tuggle, Penny Tuggle and Amy Sinnott
Interior design: eBookBurner Technologies
Publishing services provided by BelieversBookServices.com
First printing: 2024

Printed in the United States of America

ACKNOWLEDGMENTS

This book is the culmination of 17 years of learning, growing, and inspiring, all of which would not have been possible without the incredible individuals who have been part of my journey as a business coach.

First and foremost, I extend my heartfelt gratitude to my clients. Your trust and openness have allowed me to learn from you, be inspired by you, and gain invaluable insights into the world of business and personal growth. Thank you for inviting me into your lives and businesses and sharing your dreams, challenges, and successes. Your courage and dedication have been a constant source of motivation and have enriched my coaching experience beyond measure.

I also want to acknowledge the support and encouragement from my family, friends, and colleagues. Your unwavering belief in my vision and continuous support have been instrumental in my journey.

To my readers, thank you for embarking on this journey with me. I hope this book guides and inspires you to unlock your potential and achieve the success you deserve.

Lastly, to everyone who has ever been part of my life and career, know that your impact has been profound. This book is a testament to the collective experiences, lessons, and inspirations gathered over the years. I am deeply grateful to each and every one of you.

With love and gratitude,

Angie

Angie

TABLE OF CONTENTS

Let the Journey Begin

INTRODUCTION:
THE JOURNEY BEGINS

When I was in the second grade, my teacher told me I would be a success if I went to college. At age seven, I didn't really understand success, but it sounded like something I wanted. From that day forward, I planned to go to college. There were many hurdles along the way to earning that degree, including finding a way to pay the tuition, finding a job that would support me, and working around class hours. With little guidance or assistance from the adults around me, I had to apply to schools, navigate interviews, and find some way to pay for school. But I was determined that no hurdle could stand in my way for long. For four years, I worked a full-time job and attended classes full time. At times, I was exhausted, sometimes I was hungry, and always I was busy. And I did it! I earned my degree and was ready for success.

Next, I did what many of us do, what society programs us to do, and entered the corporate world and started chasing success. I worked hard and received regular promotions, climbing the ladder one step at a time. With each step, victory seemed a little closer and still farther away. Yes, I was making more money, had a job title people respected, and worked for well-known industry leaders whose names impressed people when they asked. And still, I was surrounded by people more successful than I was. They made more, had more, achieved more, and set an example that perpetually grew more difficult to match.

An unexpected event occurred almost twenty years into climbing this never-ending ladder of achieving success. My father had a health crisis and needed me to take a leave of absence from my job and my life to help him recover. During that summer, I discovered another version of a successful life: a life not driven by a need to earn more, get the next promotion, or hit a constantly growing sales target. It was about slowing down, enjoying each day, and loving the life I had versus wanting a life I might never actually achieve. Have you ever paused to question the version of success you're chasing?

And that began my journey of RADical success. Shortly after, I left the corporate world and started my own business, coaching business owners to succeed. Early on, I discovered that my most successful clients were not those chasing conventional measures of success: financial wealth, status, and prestige. They were the ones building legacies—establishing multi-generational businesses, creating opportunities for their children, serving their communities, and chasing dreams they had since they were children. Along the way, they achieved financial status and the freedom that entrepreneurship brings, but those weren't their primary goals. They were the means to achieve their primary goals. They have taught me much about how we view success and what it means for us.

My attempts to discover and create RADical success for myself led me down many paths. I have studied with Jack Canfield and Robert Cialdini and have read, reread, and dissected Napoleon Hill's *Law of Success in Sixteen Lessons* and many other books on the subject. I did a deep dive for a while into the work of Martin Seligman after hearing him speak at age ninety-two. I have spent thousands of hours in one-to-one conversations with hundreds of successful business owners as a coach, a peer, and a friend. I attend conferences and webinars and learn more each day. And, most days, I feel like a success! I have the resources to do the things I want and the time and freedom to do them. I have some status and impact on my social media following, clientele, and reputation. Most importantly, I seek to enjoy the journey and control my destiny every day. In this book, I share with you what I have learned about how to choose our definition of success and how to achieve it. It is at the core of the coaching I provide through my business, RAD Strategic Partners.

This book is my journey and a guide for anyone questioning the conventional path to success. It's for the dreamers and doers, especially those who feel stuck on a treadmill of achievement, that never seems to lead to true satisfaction. I write this not just as someone who has navigated these waters but as someone who has guided countless others to find and achieve their own definition of success. As you read through these ideas, which aspects resonate most with you and your path toward success? Drop me a line and let me what resonates most with your success.

Who is this book for? It's for you—the entrepreneur, the executive, the student, the seeker. If you're ready to redefine success on your terms and pursue it with passion and purpose, then join me. Let's embark on this journey to RADical success together, learning to achieve and appreciate the journey itself. Through my journey, and the lessons shared in this book, you'll discover how to redefine and achieve success to align with your deepest values and aspirations, one actionable step at a time.

A quick note about how to read this book: in some ways it is a DIY book that you use to look up a topic and learn how to fix what's broken in your world. And after reading it all the way through, I encourage you to keep it handy and use it that way. However, it is also, as I have been saying, a guidebook for a journey. The fifty-two-weeks' worth of topics, tips, and action steps are ordered very intentionally. I encourage you to work your way through from Week 1 through Week 52 in order. Doing so will ensure you don't miss a crucial building block that may be necessary for a future step. Now let's begin! We will start by crafting our definition of success.

THE RAD BLUEPRINT: REDEFINING SUCCESS

Success

A Dictionary Approach

/sək'ses/
noun

1. The accomplishment of an aim or purpose.
2. The satisfactory completion of something.
3. The gaining of wealth, respect, or fame.

A RADical Approach

1. The joyful mastery of bringing your unique talents to the world.
2. The continuous unfolding of your ever-expanding potential.
3. The serene satisfaction of knowing you've made your dent in the universe.

What is Success?

Picture me on a call with the comptroller's office, setting up an account for my company, RAD Strategic Partners. The helpful state employee at the other end surprised me by labeling himself the "opposite of success." Why? He's contentedly held the same position for over fifteen years, declining promotions and loving his modest life.

I said, "You're happy, impactful, and content. How is that not the very definition of success?" There it was—a shared moment of redefined success.

Zig Ziglar saw success as the maximum utilization of one's gifts. Bobby Unser said it's where preparation meets opportunity. Winston Churchill viewed it as failing while keeping your enthusiasm intact. And me? I define success as the art of crafting a life where your work, relationships, and inner joy exist in sublime balance.

Do You Consider Yourself Successful?

As we journey together toward RADical success, consider these thought-provoking questions:

- What does "achievement" look like to you, stripped of societal expectations?
- Is success an end state or a continuous journey for you?
- What role does happiness play in your equation for success?
- What legacy do you want to leave behind?
- Who do you want to be?
- How do you want to interact with the world?

For me, success is not just my accomplishments but the understanding that I can adapt, learn, and thrive. It's living a life aligned with my deepest values and aspirations.

Success Can be Fleeting

We live in a turbulent world where "one day you're Cinderella, and the next, you're Quasimodo," as Johnny Depp eloquently puts it. Thus, lasting success lies in the resilience of knowing that whatever happens, you've got what it takes to rise again.

Welcome to RADical success!

You're about to embark on a transformative journey with fifty-two gems of wisdom that will inspire, challenge, and equip you for lasting success. Are you ready to redefine success on your terms? Let's dive in.

Let's Dive In

Month 1

BUILD A FOUNDATION

Who Do You Want to Be?

Let's get one thing straight—whether you're a business owner, executive, employee, or savvy stockholder, the principles we'll discuss apply universally. Your job, your business, is more than just a livelihood; it's the runway for achieving your grandest aspirations. After all, success in business and life are two sides of the same golden coin.

Step one to RADical success? Nailing down who you aspire to be. Ask yourself: How will you show up in both the boardroom and the living room? What values will be your north star? What's the endgame you're gunning for?

Think of it this way: a GPS won't help unless you enter a destination. Defining your vision is like setting that crucial address in your life's GPS. And don't sweat if the coordinates shift over time; life is anything but static. With each phase—be it youth, parenting years, or your sage-like crone stage—expect your vision to evolve.

While some visions, like Walt Disney's ambition "to make people happy," can span lifetimes, most are time-bound. I typically nudge my clients to forecast ten years out, but you do you. Pick a timeline that resonates.

Up ahead, we'll delve into the bedrock principles that will set your course. From articulating your ethos to identifying your purpose, consider this your primer on the first steps toward RADical success.

Week 1

CHOOSE YOUR PRINCIPLES: GUIDING YOUR BUSINESS AND PERSONAL LIFE

In various aspects of life, we encounter sets of principles or commandments that offer a moral compass for decision-making and personal growth. From religious doctrines to secular philosophies, these guiding principles shape our values, actions, and aspirations. Similarly, establishing a set of "commandments" can define an organization's culture, values, and objectives in business. In this section, we will explore the significance of choosing our own principles and commandments, providing examples and guidance for creating a code that aligns with our desired outcomes.

Embracing Personalized Principles:

While well-known sets of principles, such as the Ten Commandments, exist as widely recognized moral frameworks, it is also essential to recognize the value of creating personalized commandments. We can develop a code that resonates with our unique vision for success, happiness, and fulfillment by tailoring these principles to our specific goals and aspirations.

Establishing Commandments for Business:

In the business world, establishing a set of commandments for our organization can provide a moral foundation and guide decision-making. Just as a business school encourages defining a vision, mission, and culture, these commandments shape the moral fiber of our business. They influence choices in hiring, risk management, and pursuit of opportunities, ensuring consistency and alignment with our values.

Striking a Balance:

To create a well-rounded set of commandments, it is important to establish a balance between principles governing our business's operations and those reflecting its impact on our personal lives. While the primary focus may be on business success, acknowledging and nurturing the connection between work and personal life helps maintain a fulfilling and harmonious existence.

Examples of Commandments for Business Operations:

To inspire your own commandments, here are a few examples that encompass aspects of respect, growth, quality, enjoyment, and excellence:

- We will treat our customers with unwavering respect and courtesy.
- We will cultivate a nurturing work environment that fosters the growth and well-being of our team members.
- We will strive daily to create superior products or services, avoiding shortcuts in the pursuit of profit.
- We will prioritize daily enjoyment and foster a positive work culture.
- We will achieve industry dominance through exceptional service, innovative ideas, and a proactive attitude.

Examples of Commandments for Personal Life Integration:

Consider incorporating these commandments to ensure a balanced and fulfilling personal life within the context of your business:

- I will maintain an overall balance that enriches my personal and professional lives.
- I will work diligently to create opportunities for leisure and recreation.
- I will dedicate sufficient effort to generate the time and resources necessary to live the life of my dreams.
- I will build a business that can provide for my family for generations to come.
- I will involve my family in the business in ways that are meaningful and beneficial for us.

Implementation and Reminders:

Once we have defined our commandments, we must keep them visible and regularly reinforce their importance. Consider engraving them in stone for a timeless reminder, or utilize vinyl letters, desktop objects, and screen savers for a modern touch. The key is ensuring everyone involved in our business knows and aligns with these principles.

Choosing our principles allows us to establish a moral framework for our business and personal life. By defining our commandments, we create a code that guides decision-making, nurtures growth, and fosters balance. Embrace the power of personalized principles, and let them be the compass that propels us toward success, happiness, and fulfillment.

Choosing your principles is the first step towards building a solid foundation for success. Once you have identified your core principles, the next essential step is to live by these values. This alignment between your beliefs and actions creates a strong ethos that guides your decisions and behaviors, ensuring that you stay true to yourself and your goals

Your Blueprint for Action: Turning Principles into Practice

Fantastic! You've digested the essence of choosing principles to guide both your business and personal life. Feeling inspired? Great! Let's translate this newfound wisdom into action.

Action Item:

1. Grab a notebook or open a digital document—whichever medium helps your creativity flow.
2. List three commandments you want to implement in your business. Next to each, write down one immediate step to integrate it into your daily operations.
3. Do the same for your personal life—list three commandments and the steps to make them a reality.

Now, you're probably wondering: why only three? Well, as we like to say at RAD Strategic Partners, quality trumps quantity. Three well-executed commandments can have a far greater impact than a dozen forgotten ones.

You've now set the wheels in motion. By identifying and integrating these principles, you're not just crafting a moral compass—you're shaping a strategic roadmap for your RADical success journey. Cheers to a life and business well-guided!

Week 2

DEFINE YOUR ETHOS:
THE HEARTBEAT OF VALUE IN YOUR BUSINESS

Ethos is a term not only rich in meaning but also resonating with the core values of a business or an individual. It's more than a philosophy; it's the pulse, the heartbeat, and the soul that gives life to your vision. Have you paused to feel this pulse lately? Are you dancing to its beat? If not, join us in understanding why this concept is more than an ancient Greek term but a RADical key to success.

Building your ethos starts with the seamless integration of work and life, where aligning our values allows us to be our full selves both at work and at home. When our values are in harmony, we can make better decisions and experience greater satisfaction in all aspects of our lives. This alignment ensures that we are not living fragmented lives but are instead weaving a coherent tapestry where personal and professional realms support and enhance each other. By living our values consistently, we create a strong ethos that guides our decisions and behaviors, ensuring that we stay true to ourselves and our goals.

Understanding and defining the ethos of your business isn't a task relegated to a five-minute brainstorming session. It's the foundation upon which giants are built, and dreams are achieved. It's the roadmap guiding you through the maze of entrepreneurship.

Vision and Mission Statements: Here is where your ethos starts to take form. These aren't just words to make your website look smart;

they're your compass. Simon Sinek wrote a compelling book that ignites our thoughts about the power of "why." And trust us, it's not just because he likes asking questions.

Corporate Values: Visit the jobs page of Zappos, and you will find their core values—the first of which is delivering happiness. Yours might be delivering pizzas with a smile, but what matters is that it's authentic to your business.

Why Invest in Defining Ethos?

Is it worth it? In a word, absolutely! The benefits are as vast as your entrepreneurial dreams. It's your guide to attracting the right people and measuring the worthiness of opportunities. Ethos isn't just about good vibes; it's the backbone of strategic decisions.

Crafting Your Ethos—Where to Begin:

Here's where we roll up our sleeves and dive into the art of creating an ethos that mirrors your aspirations:

- **Identify Categories:** What does your business purpose do for the world? For your customers? For your team? For you? And most importantly, for your legacy?
- **Write It Down:** Take the time to pen your ethos, and don't just shove it in a drawer. Let it breathe; let it live. Embrace it like your morning coffee.
- **Use It Wisely:** Employ your ethos in forming partnerships, achieving goals, and fulfilling opportunities. Let it be your roadmap, not just a fancy word.

Your Ethos Is Calling; Are You Answering?

Defining and living your ethos is more than an exercise; it's a lifestyle. It's choosing the path that aligns with your values. Otherwise, you risk letting others dictate your direction, and let's be honest, that's like allowing someone else to choose your outfit for a big event— risky and potentially embarrassing.

Action Item: Ethos Clarity Audit

Grab a notebook or open a digital doc. Write "Ethos" at the top, and let's begin our symphonic masterpiece.

1. **Current Ethos Elements:** Write down any existing mission, vision, or value statements. Don't be surprised if this brings a tear to your eye or an "aha!" to your lips.
2. **Authenticity:** On a scale of 1–10, how closely do these statements resonate with the current state of your business? If the scale tips below 7, my friend, you might need a remix.
3. **Core Values:** List 3–5 values that you'd consider the heartbeat of your business. Are these evident in your existing ethos elements? If not, consider this your cue for a rewrite.
4. **Future Mapping:** Now that you're in tune, how will these core values guide your strategy for the next quarter? Identify at least one initiative that will bring your ethos to life.
5. **Stakeholder Alignment:** Share your refined ethos and upcoming initiative with your team. Are they snapping their fingers in agreement or scratching their heads in confusion? Take note and refine.

Why engage in this ethos clarity audit? Simple. Just as a thriving ethos can be your north star, a neglected one can steer you into the Bermuda Triangle of business—bewildering and challenging to navigate. With this action item, we're ensuring you have a compass that's both accurate and authentically yours. Your ethos isn't just your playlist; it's your anthem, your rallying cry. Consider this your backstage pass to curating an ethos that truly rocks. Welcome to your path of RADical success.

Week 3

THE FIVE STEPS TO RADICAL SUCCESS: A RECIPE TO SPICE UP YOUR BUSINESS

Everyone loves a good secret sauce, especially when it comes to success. After years of working with the bigwigs and devouring books like a starving entrepreneur at a buffet, I've cooked up the five essential ingredients for RADical success. Grab your notebook and a fancy pen; it's time to stir up some success!

1. **Identify Your Purpose: Your Life's Flavor Enhancer**
   Why did you choose your business? Is it for fame, fortune, or the endless supply of free office coffee? Whatever the reason, discovering your purpose is like finding the perfect seasoning. Once you've got it, everything just tastes better. Your vision can be as ever-changing as your favorite playlist, guiding you through various stages of life. No purpose yet? It's time to go on a taste-test journey within yourself. Finding that unique flavor might be the secret sauce to success and longevity.

2. **Identify, Create, or Follow a System: The Business Cookbook**
   Sure, you can wing it and hope for the best, but why reinvent the wheel? Others have written recipe books for success; you only need to follow them. Identify the systems that suit your palate and apply them with gusto. Struggling with cold-calling or networking? Fear not!

There are as many guides and tips out there as there are fish in the sea. Time to go fishing for those that suit your taste.

3. **Practice Affirmations, Visualization, and Mindfulness: Your Success Meditation Menu**

Want that dream car or that corner office? Picture it and add a sprinkle of positive affirmations. Voila! You're cooking with gas. Creating a vivid mental image of success is like adding the perfect garnish to your dish. And don't worry, it's not magic; it's mindfulness. From affirmations to visualization, these techniques are as vital to your success as a chef's knife is to a kitchen.

4. **Find and Express Your Passion: The RADical Spice**

If your job feels like eating plain toast every day, it might be time to add some zest. Finding your passion makes business not just palatable but delicious. Success without passion is like a bland stew, and nobody wants to eat that. Life is too short to endure tasteless toil. Find what spices your life and sprinkle it generously.

5. **Focus More on Service than Yourself: The Customer's Plate**

Who are you serving: yourself or your customers? Focusing on delivering quality rather than gorging on personal goals ensures that the rewards will flow to you like gravy. Listening to others and genuinely catering to their needs sets you on the right culinary path. After all, in the kitchen of success, selfless service tastes better.

These five steps aren't just a recipe for RADical success; they are your secret ingredients to create a deliciously satisfying life and business. So put on your chef's hat, whip out those utensils, and start cooking up your dream future.

Remember, success doesn't happen in a microwave; it takes time, effort, and the right mix of flavors. Bon appétit, fellow business chefs!

Action Item: The RADical Success Recipe Workbook

Open up your preferred note-taking tool and title the page "Five Steps to RADical Success."

1. **Purpose Identification:** Write down what drives you—your "why" behind the "what." If you draw a blank, schedule a self-discovery session in your calendar.
2. **System Audit:** List the systems you currently have in place and rate their effectiveness on a scale of 1–10. If anything scores below a 7, it's time to spice things up.
3. **Meditation Menu:** Create a short list of affirmations and visualizations that align with your business goals. Dedicate 5–10 minutes each morning to this mental mise en place.
4. **Passion Infusion:** Are you still jazzed about your business? If not, identify areas that could use some zest. Think of an initiative or project that would reinvigorate your professional life.
5. **Service Evaluation:** Take an honest look at your customer reviews or feedback. What are you serving up, and how is it being received? Make necessary adjustments and remember, the customer's plate is always right.

Why embark on this culinary adventure? Because much like a five-course meal, each step builds on the previous one, creating a feast of RADical success. By breaking it down into actionable bites, you're making this recipe not just digestible but downright delectable.

Here at RAD Strategic Partners, we know that success isn't instant ramen; it's more like a slow-cooked stew—rich and worth the wait. So, let's get that pot simmering, shall we?

Week 4

SET BREAKTHROUGH GOALS: TRANSFORMING YOUR BUSINESS AND LIFE

Have you ever contemplated that one monumental goal capable of catalyzing tremendous change in both your business and personal life? What type of goal might have initially appeared too daunting or colossal to set? It's time to make that goal a priority. When we set our sights on a genuine breakthrough goal, we propel ourselves upward on the ladder of success.

A breakthrough goal isn't merely a destination; it's a transformational journey that can lead us to new places and turn us into entirely new individuals. We must evolve into more to attain more, accomplish more, influence more, live more, build more, and create more. The path to change is marked by discomfort, and setting our breakthrough goal into motion propels us toward our future selves.

Examples of breakthrough goals are as diverse as they are inspiring. They could involve launching, selling, or franchising a business, embarking on a new career path, relocating to a foreign country, or starting a family. These dreams guide our future and become the fuel for our ambitions.

My clients and I have achieved numerous breakthrough goals over the years. From selling a business to a significant investor, to planning a move to a foreign country, to hitting the elusive million-dollar sales mark and doubling revenues, these goals demanded focus, meticulous planning, and decisive action. Yet, they also required something deeper—transformation. Becoming an entrepreneur, a multinational entity, or an owner of a million-dollar enterprise demanded growth into new realms, experiences, and abilities.

So, what's your current breakthrough goal? Ours revolves around building a retreat center and relocating to Todos Santos, Mexico. Since setting this goal in motion, we've transformed into landowners, navigating the intricacies of a new language, becoming versed in the metric system, assuming roles as trustees, and much more. What are you prepared to become to realize your breakthrough goal?

Setting such a goal is a monumental step, but it's merely the first in a series. Now, we must chart a course to make it a reality. An excellent starting point is sharing our goals with others. Doing so not only holds us accountable but also opens doors to those who can assist in achieving our objectives. We can privately declare our goals to friends, teams, audiences, and social circles. The more we share our destination, the more opportunities emerge to make it a reality.

The next step is to look candidly at our current circumstances and discern what must change to reach our goal. Is it a need for a larger team, additional space, a strategic partnership, more knowledge, or new skills? For instance, our pursuit of the retreat center necessitates all of the above, and we've been systematically acquiring them along the way. What resources and changes are essential for you to realize your goal?

With the broader picture in sight, it's time for commitment. Consistently taking one small step each day, week, or month catalyzes progress. Daily advancement becomes second nature when we break our substantial goals into smaller, manageable steps. The monumental leap is daunting, but a sequence of small steps can lead us to the same destination, often more swiftly and with superior results. Committing to regular forward motion yields transformative results.

When we challenge ourselves to achieve something entirely unprecedented and pledge to do whatever it takes, magic ensues. It won't be a walk in the park and won't transpire overnight, but the rewards are boundless. Today, let's set our sights on a breakthrough goal.

As we conclude our discussion on achieving breakthrough goals, it becomes evident that setting ambitious targets is only the beginning of the journey. These lofty aspirations require more than just vision and determination; they demand a structured and meticulous plan to turn them into reality. The connection between setting these significant goals and the necessity of detailed planning cannot be overstated. Planning provides the roadmap that guides us from our current state to our desired destination, ensuring that our efforts are focused, strategic, and effective. In the next section, we'll explore the power of planning and how it serves as the essential bridge between our goals and their successful realization.

Ready to Set Your Breakthrough Goal? Take Action Now!

You've read about the transformative power of setting a breakthrough goal, and you're inspired to embark on this exciting journey. But where do you begin? Here's a simple yet powerful action item to get you started:

Action Item: Grab a notebook or open a digital document. Write down the most significant breakthrough goal you've been hesitant to set. This goal can propel you to new heights in your business and life. Now, beside this goal, jot down why achieving it is crucial to you—what impact will it have?

Next, follow these steps:

1. **Break It Down:** Divide your breakthrough goal into smaller, manageable milestones. What are the key steps you need to take to reach it? Write them down.
2. **Set a Timeline:** Assign a realistic time frame to each milestone. When do you aim to achieve it? Be specific.
3. **Seek Accountability:** Share your goals and milestones with someone you trust—a friend, a mentor, a family member, or a colleague. They can help keep you on track and offer support and encouragement.
4. **Acquire Resources:** Identify what resources, skills, or knowledge you might need to reach your goal. Make a list of these requirements.
5. **Take the First Step:** Commit to taking action today. It might be a small step, but it's a crucial one. Your journey begins with this single action.

You're transforming a vision into a concrete plan by breaking down your breakthrough goal into actionable steps and setting a clear path forward. Remember, achieving a breakthrough goal requires commitment and perseverance, but the rewards are immeasurable. Your future self will thank you for taking this first step today.

Month 2

TAKE ACTION

Getting Things Done: The Art of RADical Execution

You've got your vision and principles on lock—fantastic! But what separates a dream from reality is the act of doing, my friends. This section is where the rubber meets the road, the espresso meets the early morning, and, let's be honest, where the excuses come to die.

Consider this section your toolbox for RADical execution—a collection of actionable strategies, tips, and "let's do this" mantras designed to translate your aspirations into achievements. We'll delve into the secrets of effective prioritization, the psychology of procrastination (and how to give it the boot), and the little hacks that can make a big difference in your daily productivity.

Whether you're a CEO wondering how to lead your team to the next big thing or an individual contemplating how to make your life's vision a reality, it's all about action. As they say, even a Tesla needs a good jolt to get going.

Ready to shift from contemplating to conquering? Let's dive into RADical execution because success isn't just about knowing the path; it's about walking it.

Week 5

SMALL STEPS MAKE GREAT STRIDES: ACHIEVING YOUR LOFTIEST GOALS

Climbing a ladder with two out of every three rungs missing would seem impossible. The steps are just too big. Often, we face similar obstacles when striving to build our businesses and create radical lives. Our loftiest goals and dreams may appear daunting, and even taking the first step can seem overwhelming. We don't know how to create something we've never made before, and we can't find the rungs to get us to our goals. Each step feels too large.

The answer lies in taking small steps consistently. Great strides come from small actions taken every day. Our journeys to success are the result of thousands of small steps along the way. By viewing our future in this way, we gain control by choosing daily steps.

So, how do we eat an elephant? One bite at a time. The same principle applies to reaching our loftiest goals. Getting from here to there is not a giant leap but a series of actions. Starbucks didn't appear on every corner overnight; they opened those stores one by one. Day by day, action by action, we can accomplish anything.

The small-step strategy works for all areas of our lives, whether we're building companies, taking control of our health, or even increasing our walking pace. Small steps are the way to make significant changes.

A Five-Step Method for Making Great Strides Through Small Steps:

1. **Choose a Goal:** Start by selecting a goal. What is one thing you need to accomplish in the coming year? Choosing one primary goal each year and committing to the necessary actions is a powerful way to move forward with intention and achieve results.
2. **List the Steps You Know:** Frequently, we don't have all the information we need to make our dreams come true. That's okay! You can learn what you need to know and employ experts to fill in the gaps. Each step you take will reveal new information. Begin with the steps you know.
3. **Make the Steps Small:** To take a step every day, make it manageable, and ensure there are enough rungs for you to climb the ladder.
4. **Repeat Steps When Needed:** Repetition is key. The same action repeated over and over will take you far. When you practice, repeat, and refine, your efforts become more powerful.
5. **Take a Step Every Day:** Just as you can't climb a ladder without moving up the rungs, you can't reach your goals without taking consistent steps toward them. Commit to an ongoing series of small steps.

Many steps cover great distances, not one giant leap. The same principle applies to your goals. Keep moving, step by step, in the direction of your dreams, and watch them come true.

Embracing the Power of Small Steps:

The essence of this strategy is not only about making progress but also about gaining momentum. Each small step you take reinforces your commitment to your goals. It transforms a seemingly insurmountable challenge into a series of achievable tasks. The journey to success is no longer a daunting leap but a collection of small strides.

Remember, the road to success is paved with consistent effort and determination. Small steps may seem inconsequential on their own, but collectively, they form the path to your loftiest goals. Embrace the power of small steps, and you'll find yourself making great strides toward the life and success you desire.

Small steps every day

Action Item: The Daily Small-Step Challenge

1. **Select a Goal:** Choose one of your loftiest goals or dreams that you want to work toward. It could be related to your career, personal life, health, or any area you want to improve.
2. **Identify One Small Step:** Break down this big goal into the smallest possible action you can take today. This step should be so small that it feels almost effortless. For example, if your goal is to write a book, your small step could be writing just one sentence or brainstorming a book title.
3. **Commit to Daily Action:** Every day, commit to taking that small step, no matter how busy or challenging your day may be. Make it a non-negotiable part of your daily routine.
4. **Track Your Progress:** Create a simple tracking system, like a checklist or a calendar, to mark off each day that you successfully complete your small step.
5. **Reflect and Adjust:** At the end of each week or month, take a moment to reflect on your progress. Celebrate your consistency and the small victories along the way.
6. **Gradually Increase Complexity:** As you build momentum and confidence, gradually increase the complexity of your daily small step. The key is to keep it manageable but challenging enough to move you closer to your larger goal.

By taking these small daily steps, you're not only making progress toward your loftiest goals, but you're also building a habit of consistent action. Over time, these small actions will compound, leading you to achieve what once seemed like an insurmountable dream. Remember, great strides are the result of small, consistent efforts.

Week 6

ACHIEVE ANYTHING: THE RADICAL FIFTEEN-MINUTE SYSTEM FOR SUCCESS

How many times have you said to yourself, "I would like to get [insert task] done, but I just cannot find the time?" Do you have any projects that have been waiting for completion for weeks, months, or even years? Most people find it exceedingly difficult to carve out sufficient time to accomplish all the tasks they want and need to do. We always tend to have some long-term project that is important but not urgent. There is always something, whether it is creating a great marketing plan, cleaning out our digital file cabinets, scanning family photos, or donating old kids' clothes. Finding an extra day, week, or even a few hours to complete a long-term task can be challenging. Our schedules are busy, our time is valuable, and that someday becomes never. Finding big chunks of time to complete projects is just too hard. But what about fifteen minutes? Most days, we waste at least fifteen minutes, and it is not that hard to find this small chunk of time real estate.

Let's be honest. We will always have some significant long-term tasks we need to complete. Even if we manage to keep up with the day to day, the world changes and those changes create projects. New technology, new opportunities, new media, and new ideas constantly generate the need to clean up, clean out, and upgrade. These essential tasks improve our productivity and lives once completed, but they are not necessarily time sensitive from a deadline perspective. Frequently, they are time sensitive from an investment perspective. They may take hours, days, or even longer to complete, and we will never find that kind of time.

The RADical Secret Is Fifteen Minutes:

1. **Step 1 is finding fifteen minutes in your day.** Where do you look for the time? There are many places you can find an extra fifteen minutes. Some of them include the time between appointments, waiting for return calls, general waiting time, getting up fifteen minutes earlier, going to bed fifteen minutes later, or even the time spent in the car while sitting at red lights. You get the idea. Now consider your day and reflect on the places where those fifteen minutes might be hiding.

2. **Step 2 is learning to complete any task in fifteen minutes.** "Impossible!" you might say. But no, it's entirely doable. Let me share a story with you. I met a remarkably busy man who ran marathons a long time ago. When I asked how he found time to train, he told me that he carried his running gear everywhere and ran anytime there was a wait of fifteen minutes or more. He trained for a marathon in fifteen minutes! Fifteen minutes a day, that is. Similarly, Rick Bradley of Rick's Quick Fit1 has a training program that requires only fifteen minutes daily to maintain physical fitness. According to him, the secret is that it's fifteen minutes every day. One secret to RADical success is accomplishing anything when you consistently commit fifteen minutes to work toward your goal. The time is not the secret; the consistency is.

---

[1] https://www.quickfitkit.com/

3. **Step 3 is deciding what you want to accomplish.** Do you want to run a marathon, write a business plan, create a marketing calendar, put together employee manuals, or learn a foreign language? You can build a company, train for a new career, create a legacy, or clean out a basement. Whatever it is, you can do it if you just devote fifteen minutes daily.

4. **Step 4 is being prepared.** The key to making this work is to prepare for your fifteen-minute block. You must have the materials ready so you can make the most of the minutes when you find them. You should always carry a book if you are trying to read more business books. I read the daily newspaper by keeping it in my car and reading it at red lights or while waiting for appointments. Once you have determined when your fifteen-minute block will be, gather your materials and have them ready. There are many technical tools for making this easy. Dropbox2 is an excellent resource for making computer files portable and easily accessible. An iPad or tablet can be a great way to carry materials with you. A spiral or other notebook works just as well. If you are going to run a marathon, always have your shoes with you. Once you have determined the time and gathered the materials, you are ready to go.

Now, give it a try, and you will be amazed! I have had many clients put this into practice, and 100 percent of them have had success. I have used this technique to downsize two households, digitize all my paper files, learn Spanish, and more. Once you master it, you can do anything in just fifteen minutes a day.

---

[2] www.dropbox.com

Action Item:

Grab your preferred note-taking tool and identify one long-term project or goal you've been putting off. Now, break that mammoth task down into smaller, fifteen-minute actionable tasks. These could be as simple as "write the intro paragraph for the business plan" or "sort one drawer of old papers."

Why are we doing this? At RAD Strategic Partners, we know that the bridge between intention and completion is paved with fifteen-minute blocks. By dissecting your larger goal into manageable portions, you're creating a roadmap for your RADical success journey. It's not just about dreaming big; it's about acting small, consistently.

Once you have your list, find a fifteen-minute slot in your day and tackle the first task. Then, make it a habit. It's just like brushing your teeth, but with possibly less minty freshness and more life-altering potential.

There you go—fifteen minutes to a RADically better you. How's that for a time investment?

Week 7

CHOOSE YOUR TIME ZONE: MAXIMIZING LIFE'S MOST VALUABLE ASSET

What's the world's most precious commodity? While traditional economists peg data as today's gold, I'm throwing my hat in for another contender—time. As we like to say at RAD Strategic Partners, understanding the value of time is the first step toward achieving RADical success.

The Finite Nature of Time:

The reality is that time, unlike data, money, or even a rhinoceros horn, is nonrenewable. Once it's gone, it's gone. You can't mine, drill, or crowdfund it back into existence. Whether we're CEOs, solopreneurs, or in between, each of us has twenty-four hours to work with, and no power on Earth can change that. To truly elevate our businesses and lives, we must become masters of our own "time zones."

The Four Time Zones of Life:

Effectively managing your "time zones" can drastically reduce stress, increase your ability to achieve goals, and raise your overall life satisfaction. We can categorize our daily activities into four waking time zones:

Time Zone	Description	Strategy to Improve
Pressure Zone	Tasks we do now because they are due now.	Prioritize and plan ahead.
Procrastination Zone	Tasks we do now to avoid what we should be doing.	Identify triggers; set mini-goals.
Pleasure Zone	Tasks we do now for immediate satisfaction.	Balance with productivity goals.
Productivity Zone	Tasks we do now for future benefits.	Align with long-term objectives.

The Nature of Procrastination:

While we can theoretically control our time in each zone, some zones, like procrastination, seem hardwired into human behavior. In a study by psychologist Piers Steel, up to 95 percent of people admit to procrastination.[3] It's virtually a universal experience. Procrastination is like the universe saying, "Take five, you've earned it!" So, while we can strive to minimize our time here, entirely eliminating it might be wishful thinking.

Pleasure Through Productivity:

Contrary to popular belief, the pleasure zone isn't about evading work—quite the opposite. A 2013 study published in The Journal of Positive Psychology found that people who engage in meaningful, productive activities report feeling happier and more fulfilled.[4]

---

[3] https://www.academia.edu/25615827/The_nature_of_procrastination
[4] Yuna L. Ferguson, Kennon M. Sheldon , "Trying to be happier really can work: Two experimental studies," *The Journal of Positive Psychology*, (2013): 8 (1)

That euphoric state where time seems to pause, and you're entirely engrossed in a task—that's your "flow." It enlarges your pleasure zone while shrinking your pressure zone.

How to Master Your Productivity Zone:

Elevating your time in the productivity zone allows your pleasure zone to grow while the pressure and procrastination zones recede. Here are some actionable strategies:

1. **Plan Ahead:** Most pressure zone tasks are urgent and essential. Planning ahead helps you delegate or tackle these tasks before they become critical. Use tools like time blocking to schedule your productivity zone activities.
2. **Leverage Skills and Talents:** Know your strengths and lean into them. If writing isn't your forte, hire a professional writer. If analytics makes your eyes glaze over, delegate it. You'll spend more time being productive, which, in turn, makes your pleasure zone that much sweeter.
3. **Manage Commitments:** When you schedule something, stick to it. Keeping commitments is not just good ethics; it's excellent time management.

In conclusion, mastering your time zones isn't merely a lofty ambition; it's a tangible goal anyone can achieve. The secret sauce? Planning, self-discipline, and a laser focus on the productivity zone. So, are you ready to transform your relationship with time and rocket towards RADical success? If so, the action item below is your launchpad. Fasten your seatbelts; it's going to be a thrilling ride.

Action Item: Unlock Your Productivity Zone

Here are your immediate next steps.

1. Write down one task that constantly lands in your pressure zone and one in your procrastination zone.
2. Next to each task, pinpoint why it finds itself in that zone. Is it due to poor planning, lack of skills, or something else?
3. Brainstorm and jot down at least one strategy to shift each task into your productivity zone.
4. Transform these strategies into a concrete action plan for the next thirty days.

Why are we doing this? As we say at RAD Strategic Partners, mastering your "time zones" is your first step toward RADical success. By identifying time wasters and creating an action plan, you're not just daydreaming—you're devising a roadmap for RADical success. So, what are you waiting for? Grab that notepad, and let's transform those time zones.

Week 8

TAKE ACTION EVERY DAY: THE MASTER KEY TO ACHIEVING RADICAL SUCCESS

If you're looking for that one magic formula for success in business and life, we have it right here: take consistent daily action. Forget about the "someday syndrome," where you promise to start "someday." At RAD Strategic Partners, we believe in taking actionable steps now. Let's dive in and see how you can build your success, one action at a time.

What Does It Mean to "Take Action Every Day"?

Simply put, "taking action" means doing something—anything—that brings you closer to your life and business goals. Researching, brainstorming, reaching out to prospective clients, and working on a business proposal are all actions. It's not about grand gestures but taking consistent, small daily steps, even when you don't feel like it.

The Importance of Consistency:

Consistency is king when it comes to taking action. The twenty-four-hour cycle we call a day should involve some time dedicated to your vision and values, no matter how small. Planning and intentionality should never take a back seat, whether you're on vacation or simply enjoying a day off. If you let the world dictate your pace, you'll end up somewhere far from where you want to be.

The Perks of Taking Action:

- **Apply Knowledge:** Information is powerful, but it's the application that truly serves us.
- **Streamline Methods:** Taking action helps you identify what's not working, allowing you to focus on what does work.
- **Create Success Habits:** Starting is the hardest part. Once you take that step, habit formation takes over and carries you towards your goals.
- **Normalize Achievement:** Every action validates your journey and brings a sense of accomplishment.

Theories That Back Up Daily Actions:

The Japanese concept of kaizen speaks of continuous improvement through small steps. Jack Canfield's Rule of Five suggests doing five things daily to reach your goal. Newton's first law tells us that an object at rest stays at rest, and an object in motion stays in motion. Or, as Pablo Picasso said, "Action is the foundational key to all success."

What's Holding You Back?

The enemies of action are time, confusion, lethargy, and fear. But the most insidious is the lack of a plan. Once you commit, your next step is to lay out an actionable plan.

Crafting Your Action Plan: A Quick Guide:

1. **Set Current Goals:** Zero in on 2–5 goals crucial for your RADical success.
2. **List Necessary Steps:** Break down into manageable steps, be it a business plan or a household task.
3. **Identify Roadblocks:** Pinpoint what you need but don't yet have and make acquiring those a part of your action plan.
4. **Be Prepared:** Ensure you have all the resources you need.
5. **Commit:** Decide on the frequency and extent of your actions.

Time to Get Started:

There's no better time than now. As you engage with these strategies, you'll find your roadblocks turning into stepping stones. Before you know it, your RADical dreams and goals will have transformed from aspiration to reality.

Ready to Act? Here's Your Action Item:

So, you're pumped and primed to take daily actions for your RADical success. What's your immediate next step? Simple.

Action Item: Grab a notebook or open up a digital note. Write down one goal you've been putting off for weeks, months, or even years. Next to it, jot down a tiny action you can take today to move closer to that goal. Finally, set a reminder to take that small action at a specific time today.

Why are we doing this? At RAD Strategic Partners, we firmly believe in turning intentions into implementations. Your action isn't just a checkbox—it's the beginning of a chain reaction. By identifying and transforming your procrastinated goals into actionable steps, you're not just dreaming; you're doing. And doing, as we've established, is the foundation of your RADical success journey.

Week 9

JUST GET IT DONE: MASTERING PRODUCTIVITY TO TAKE CONTROL OF YOUR TIME FOR SUCCESS

In the bustling corridors of modern business, time is not just money; it's the golden ticket to success. Ah, the elusive twenty-fifth hour of the day. We've all searched for it, but as any savvy entrepreneur knows, it's like looking for a vegan at a barbecue—darn near impossible. So what's the secret sauce? The key lies not in attempting to manage time itself but in managing ourselves effectively. Adopting a self-management mindset can unlock our true potential and maximize our productivity.

Managing Yourself, Not Time: A Journey to Productivity

Hold your horses; we're not selling time travel here (though I'm sure that's a marketable business idea). No, recognizing that we cannot manage time is the first step toward achieving productivity mastery. Forget about wrestling with the clock and start focusing on managing yourself. Deciding to take action rather than falling into the black hole of constant planning will allow you to make significant progress toward your goals. Like every diet plan, it's all about taking the first step.

The Power of Choice and Action: Becoming the Captain of Your Destiny:

Remember when choosing between two different types of coffee was your biggest decision? Me neither. In the world of business, every choice can be a game changer. Start by defining the desired outcome and break it down into actionable steps. This isn't a cake recipe, but breaking complex tasks into smaller parts still leads to something sweet—success!

Unlocking Time: Freeing Up Resources Like a Wizard with a Time-Turner:

While we can't create time (unless you're a wizard hiding from us mere Muggles), we can optimize its use. Evaluate how you spend your time and consider areas to reduce or eliminate. Maybe cut down on cat videos (I know, it's hard) or outsource some daily tasks. By decluttering our schedules, we make room for the golden nuggets—the activities that align with our goals.

Taking Control and Embracing Accountability: The Adulting Part:

Ah, the dreaded "A" word—accountability. It's the real key to unlocking productivity. Stop blaming time like it's some mischievous elf stealing your hours. Recognize that we're in control of our actions and choices. Once we start adulting in the productivity department, obstacles crumble like a cookie in a toddler's hand.

Grabbing Success by the Horns:

In the wild rodeo of productivity, shift your focus from managing time to managing yourself. Understand that action, choice, and accountability are the triple threat required to break free from procrastination. So, slap on a smile, roll up those sleeves, and commit to "just get it done." With this newfound mindset, the possibilities for personal and professional growth are not just endless; they're practically lining up to shake your hand.

Now go out there and show time who's boss! And remember, as with any good business strategy, it's always wise to keep an eye on the clock but let your goals set the pace.

Action Item:

Take out your calendar, whether it's a physical planner or a digital one, and allocate a consistent fifteen-minute block every day for what we'll call "RADical action time."

Why are we doing this? In the realm of RAD Strategic Partners, we understand that success is a daily practice. By dedicating a fifteen-minute block each day to take one tangible step towards your goals, you're not just flirting with success; you're entering a committed relationship with it.

This is your time to:

- send that important email you've been putting off;
- research a competitor's new strategy;
- take a micro-course to brush up on a new skill;
- reach out to a potential client or partner.

By consistently doing this, you accumulate what we like to call "action capital." And as we all know, in business, capital is queen. This little daily investment may seem minor, but it compounds exponentially, pushing you miles ahead in your RADical success journey.

So there you have it—a simple yet effective way to make progress a daily ritual. Because in the world of business, stagnation is the real enemy.

Month 3

ADOPT THE BEHAVIORS OF SUCCESS

Building Habits and Behaviors for RADical Success

If the first sections lay the groundwork for where you're headed, consider this section the daily regimen that gets you there. Habits and behaviors are the stepping stones on your path to RADical success. Think of them as a highly effective individual's "best practices."

Here, we go beyond mere planning and vision. We delve into the actionable, practical strategies for building a daily routine that aligns seamlessly with your goals. From crafting supporting habits to mastering RADical self-discipline, this section is all about the do's and don'ts that make success less of an aspiration and more of a daily reality.

Have you ever wondered why some people can commit to excellence as naturally as breathing? It's not magic; it's method. In this section, you'll discover how to develop a winning attitude, participate fully in your success journey, and maintain a consistent level of excellence. Because let's face it, success isn't just about reaching peaks—it's about sustaining the climb.

So, are you ready to make success a habit, not just an event? Let's dive into building the behaviors that bring your vision to life. Onward to RADical success!

Week 10

CREATE SUPPORTING HABITS:
DAILY ROUTINES TO DRIVE RADICAL SUCCESS

The saying goes, "You are what you repeatedly do. Excellence, then, is not an act but a habit." Although its attribution to Aristotle is contested, the essence of the philosophy remains spot-on for anyone pursuing success—be it in business or life.

Habits: The Silent Architects of Your Future

So let's cut to the chase: are your habits your stepping stones or stumbling blocks? Here at RAD Strategic Partners, we advocate for proactive habit formation that serves as the cornerstone of your RADical success. Because let's face it, habits form whether you're aware of them or not. Some shoot you forward like a SpaceX rocket, while others keep you orbiting in the same old space.

Evaluating Habits: Four Crucial Questions for Success

Take a GPS snapshot of your life with these four questions:

1. What activities should I do LESS of?
2. What must I STOP doing altogether?
3. What should I do MORE of?
4. What am I NOT doing that I should start?

These four questions are more than mere queries; they're your compass to effective habit formation. With honest answers, you pave your highway to RADical success. The key is to incorporate good habits into your daily routine deliberately. Planning your day, seizing opportunities, monitoring cash flow, or eating healthily—each contributes to your well-being and success in a significant way.

Beware: The Habitual Time Wasters

Conversely, we all have those sneaky habits that nibble at our productivity. Continuous email checking, doomscrolling, or watching the latest series on Netflix are often not the recreational breaks we think they are. Instead, they're habits that add zero to the bottom line of life's balance sheet.

In one of his blog posts, Seth Godin advocated for replacing such time-wasting activities with more mindful tasks.[5] Instead of scrolling through social media during your break, how about scanning those pending files that need digitization? Or better yet, replace scrolling with a quick meditation session or a brisk walk.

The Science of Habit Formation

Charles Duhigg, in his book *The Power of Habit*, lays out the cue-response-reward system that fundamentally drives our habitual behaviors. He suggests replacing ingrained responses with conscious habits that align with our objectives. Essentially, you're upgrading your routine OS to optimize rewards.

The Thirty-Day Commitment

Let's get practical. One way to embed a new habit is a thirty-day challenge. Want to get fit? Hit the gym for thirty consecutive days. Want to expand your intellect? Dedicate time to read every

---

[5] https://seths.blog/2019/02/productive-safe-harbors/

day for a month. Thirty days can transform an act into a habit. When aligned with your goals, habits become your stepping stones to success.

Your Habits, Your Success

In the grand scheme of RADical success, it's not the grand gestures but the small, repeated actions that count. Your habits are essentially your silent partners in this journey. Treat them well, choose them wisely, and watch how they transform your life and business.

So, what habit will you commit to for the next thirty days? Remember, every day is a new opportunity to make a RADical change. Choose your habits wisely; they're the architects of your future success.

30 Day Habit Commitment

Your Next Steps: Time for Action

So, you're all fueled up with insights and ready to morph your habits into your personal success team. But what's the immediate action plan? We've got you covered.

Action Item: Grab a notepad and divide it into four sections, each corresponding to one of the four crucial questions above. List your answers. Done? Pick one habit from each section that you will focus on for the next week.

Why this exercise? As we're fond of saying at RAD Strategic Partners, identifying your habits is the first step toward molding them into pillars of your RADical success. You're not just collecting insights here; you're laying down the concrete for your pathway to success.

Remember, the magic happens outside of the comfort zone. Happy habit forming!

Week 11

DEVELOP A WINNING ATTITUDE: THE KEY TO UNLOCKING YOUR FULL POTENTIAL

Success is not accidental. It's crafted, nurtured, and actualized by those who understand the fundamental importance of mindset. Yes, you heard it right—mindset. A winning attitude sets apart those who achieve their goals from those who don't. Individuals who foster a winning mindset take complete ownership of their actions and their lives. On the flip side, those who miss the mark on their goals often search externally for reasons, which are often just thinly veiled excuses. Your attitude doesn't just affect how you view the world; it impacts the results you achieve.

Three Building Blocks to a Winning Attitude

To instill this winning mindset, integrate these three processes into your daily routine:

1. **Self-Reflection Over Blame** When things don't go as planned, your first instinct might be to find external factors to blame. Stop right there. Turn the lens inward and ask yourself what you could have done differently in the same situation. We don't have control over external events or other people; we only have control over ourselves. Example:

- ○ Losing Attitude (LA): "I can't believe Susie keeps eating my yogurt. She needs to respect my property."
- ○ Winning Attitude (WA): "Susie keeps eating my yogurt. I better put it somewhere she won't find it."

2. **Be Vocal, Be Clear** How often have you waited for someone else to give you what you need? How many times has this person had absolutely no idea that you were waiting on them? Communication is key. Make your needs known. Example:
   - ○ LA: "Can't he see my arms are full, and I can't open the door? How long will I wait for that stranger to finish his call and open the door for me?"
   - ○ WA: "Excuse me, sir, could you open the door for me?"

3. **Time and Money: Two Sides of the Same Coin** Consider time and money as interchangeable resources. You can often save one by spending the other. If there's something you're not good at or don't enjoy, consider outsourcing it. Example:
   - ○ LA: "I don't know how to do X."
   - ○ WA: "I need to do X to succeed. Where can I learn how, or whom can I hire to do that?"

The Proof Is in the Pudding

According to a study by Stanford University[6], a positive attitude contributes more to success than IQ, talent, or socioeconomic status. Simply put, attitude is your secret weapon.

A Winning Attitude is Your Best Ally

A winning attitude is a catalyst. It drives our actions, fuels our ambitions, and ultimately delivers our results. When you look at

---

[6] https://journals.sagepub.com/doi/abs/10.1177/0956797617735528?-journalCode=pssa

the world through the lens of a winning attitude, barriers become stepping stones, and setbacks become setups for comebacks.

Quick Action Steps to Build Your Winning Attitude

- Survey your surroundings for annoyances and decide on actions to rectify them.
- Assess your skill set; delegate tasks that aren't your forte.
- Compile a list of tasks that could be simplified with outside help, and reach out.

By taking these small but powerful steps, we set ourselves up for success. These actions strengthen our mindset and keep us focused on progress. A winning attitude isn't just about optimism; it's about taking purposeful steps to clear our goals' path. Every decision creates the foundation for resilience, adaptability, and lasting achievement.

Take the Quiz

Action Item for RADical Success:

You're charged up and ready to develop that winning attitude. But what's the immediate next step? Simple.

Action Item: Take a moment to identify one situation where your attitude didn't serve you well. Jot down how a shift in perspective could have altered the outcome. Now, commit to applying this new mindset when a similar situation arises.

Why are we doing this? At RAD Strategic Partners, we believe fine-tuning your attitude is the stepping stone to your RADical success journey. By recognizing where you could improve and taking actionable steps, you're not just gaining insights but crafting a game plan.

Ready to evaluate your attitude for RADical success? Take our quiz now![7]

---

[7] https://www.radstrategic.com/product/how-winning-is-my-attitude

Week 12

PARTICIPATE FULL ON: EMBRACING FULL ENGAGEMENT FOR MAXIMUM IMPACT

"You get back what you put in" is a phrase we often hear in business. Let's face it, it's profoundly accurate. If you're interested in achieving RADical results in your life and career, participating full on is not an option; it's a requirement.

Full On Participation: The Core of Excellence

When coaching one-to-one or speaking to large audiences, I always request that all clients participate fully in my sessions. Doing so is a two-way street. I also center and ground myself before each engagement to ensure I'm 100 percent present. Why? Because to extract total value from any endeavor, be it a coaching session, business meeting, or strategic plan, full on participation is essential. Phoning it in simply won't cut it, and your teams are taking notes.

The Challenge of Complacency

Now, the million-dollar question: are you pulling out all the stops to skyrocket your business or career success? If the answer doesn't lead you to a resounding "yes," you need to consider what roadblocks you're hitting. What changes must you implement to elevate your game and take your business to unprecedented heights?

The Cornerstones of Full On Participation

Full on participation in the business arena encapsulates several elements:

1. **Consistency over Perfectionism:** One of the roadblocks to RADical success is the illusion of perfection. Aim to complete essential tasks every day, week, and month. Consistency trumps occasional greatness every time.

2. **Lifelong Learning:** Don't allow your knowledge to collect dust. Dive into books, podcasts, and educational videos. Keep your knowledge fresh, and your results will mirror that freshness.

3. **Timely Follow-Ups:** How many opportunities have you missed simply because you failed to follow up? Go back through your notes, calendars, and business cards. Reignite those lost opportunities with a simple call. You'll be surprised at what unfolds.

4. **Selective Commitment:** It's tempting to say "yes" to everything, but participating fully means saying "no" to commitments you can't handle, freeing you to excel in the promises you make.

5. **Accountability:** When plans derail (and they will), take full responsibility for the outcomes and make necessary adjustments. The only absolute failure is the failure to persist in reaching your goals.

The Benefits

Many studies have shown increased ownership of work, efficiency, and effectiveness when we fully participate. It's not just about feeling good; it's about bottom-line results.

Let's Turn Insight into Action

You're fired up and eager to participate fully for RADical results. So, what's the immediate action item?

Action Item: Take out your calendar and earmark a thirty-minute slot within the next week, dedicating it solely to revisiting your current commitments. Identify at least one commitment you've been dragging your feet on. Next to it, write down a realistic and immediate next step to revive it or put it to rest once and for all.

Why are we doing this? At RAD Strategic Partners, we firmly believe that full-on participation starts with revisiting commitments and making conscious decisions. By pinpointing stalled commitments and taking actionable steps, you're not just reflecting—you're charting a course for your RADical success journey.

Week 13

STRIVE FOR GOOD: CONSISTENT EXCELLENCE EVERY DAY

In the pursuit of personal and professional growth, the question often arises: should we strive to be good or great? While aiming for greatness may seem enticing, there is value in the predictability of being consistently good. This chapter explores the importance of reliability and how it can lead to long-term success and fulfillment.

Predictable Excellence

As customers, we tend to appreciate consistent experiences rather than occasional moments of brilliance. Consider the example of a restaurant: would you prefer dining at a place that delivers occasional greatness but is inconsistent overall? Most people lean towards establishments that consistently meet their expectations. We thrive on predictability, as it provides a sense of stability and comfort.

The same principle applies in the workplace. Employers often value employees who consistently perform well day after day. While sporadic bursts of greatness may be impressive, sustained excellence contributes more to meeting and exceeding expectations. A screen actor may get away with occasional brilliance, but for a Broadway hopeful, consistency is vital.

Choosing the Path of Consistency

Our society frequently sacrifices greatness for consistency. We prefer knowing what to expect and relying on familiar options. For instance, we may choose to eat at McDonald's, a reliable fast-food chain, over a restaurant that occasionally offers extraordinary meals. The equation for happiness from Tom Magliozzi[8], which states that happiness equals reality minus expectations, reinforces our inclination toward predictability.

Striving for Consistency

Many of us aspire to greatness, aiming for perfection and high standards in our interactions with others. We desire customer adoration, employee recognition, and the admiration of our loved ones. However, it is crucial to recognize that consistently failing to deliver predictable results can disappoint people. We often succeed more by striving to be consistently good rather than sporadically great. Doing so does not mean we cannot have moments of greatness; our best strategy is to be consistently good at what we do.

Building Lasting Impressions

Delivering greatness and then failing to maintain that standard can lead to disappointment. Imagine a new sandwich shop that wows you with the best sandwich you've ever tasted. You share your excitement with friends, only to be disappointed by subsequent visits that fail to match the initial experience. Each time a new bar is set, expectations rise, potentially diminishing happiness.

I had that experience at a local restaurant that shall remain nameless. They deliver a good sandwich, and many people love them. Unfortunately, the first time I ate there, I had the best sandwich I have ever enjoyed, and they have never lived up to that

---

[8] https://www.cartalk.com/blogs/staff-blog/quotable-tom-magliozzi

bar again. Knowing I will be disappointed, I no longer frequent that restaurant.

Achieving Consistent Excellence

How can we achieve the highest level of consistent excellence? Here are a few simple steps to get you started:

1. It starts with creating and implementing small systems. These systems, whether simple or more complex, help streamline our daily routines. From having consistent phone greetings to following the same route to work, small systems contribute to smooth operations.
2. The next crucial step is fulfilling our commitments. Following through on our promises is often overlooked but essential for maintaining trust and reliability. Whether making timely callbacks or honoring satisfaction guarantees, it is crucial to fulfill what we say we will do. Using calendars and schedules can be instrumental in ensuring accountability.
3. Lastly, seeking feedback and analyzing data can guide us in identifying the habits and behaviors that foster positive relationships. Being consistently good does not mean staying stagnant; it means continuously improving our level of "good" to reach new heights.

Strive for Consistency; Aim for Excellence

In conclusion, strive to be consistently good rather than inconsistently great. Embrace the value of predictability and reliability in both personal and professional spheres. Assess your current systems and develop new strategies to enhance your consistency. Commit to following through on your promises and seeking feedback to improve your relationships. Embrace the journey towards reliable and RADical success.

Action Item: Your Blueprint for Consistent Excellence

1. **System Scan:** Start by jotting down one small system you already have in place that contributes to your day running smoothly. Maybe it's how you sort your emails or a productivity app you can't live without. Label this your "consistency catalyst."

2. **Commitment Check:** Next, identify one commitment you've made recently—either in business or your personal life—that you've successfully followed through on. What strategies did you employ to ensure you fulfilled it? Note this as your commitment cornerstone.

3. **Feedback Funnel:** Consider the last piece of constructive feedback you received. How did you respond? Did you make adjustments based on this feedback? This is your feedback funnel.

4. **Next-Level Action:** Take your consistency catalyst, commitment cornerstone, and feedback funnel and translate each into a specific action step to implement this coming week. Make it achievable and SMART.

5. **Accountability, Baby:** Share these action steps with someone you trust. You're more likely to follow through when you know someone will check in. This is your accountability anchor.

At RAD Strategic Partners, we believe that embracing consistency isn't a cap on your potential—it's your ladder to RADical success. Don't misunderstand; aiming for excellence is not a crime. However, don't underestimate the powerhouse of being consistently good, for that's where trust is built and sustained. So, are you ready to take consistent action for RADical success? Because we have a feeling you're up for the challenge.

Month 4

DEVELOP A WINNING MINDSET

Mindset Matters: Cultivating a RADical Headspace for Success

Your habits and behaviors may provide the structure, but your mindset is the blueprint that shapes how you build, adapt, and grow. It's the quiet architect behind every decision and action, subtly influencing how you navigate both triumphs and challenges. In this section, we shift from the concrete actions that drive success to the intangible forces within—the mental frameworks that either propel or hinder your progress.

Consider this section your mental fitness center. Just like physical training, cultivating a success-oriented mindset requires intentional effort and practice. Here, you'll learn how to think differently, challenge old beliefs, and embrace fresh perspectives. We'll explore how meditation can sharpen your focus and reduce stress, and why happiness—yes, happiness—should be a cornerstone of your leadership approach. Drawing from the wisdom of Zen Taoism, we'll examine how ancient principles can inspire your modern-day hustle.

But mental endurance isn't just about thinking differently; it's about maintaining balance. Just as high-performance athletes need rest, so too do high-performing professionals. We'll dive into the essential practice of unplugging and recharging—because even the most ambitious among us needs time to reboot and refresh.

So, are you ready to prime your mind for lasting success? Let's unlock the mental pathways that will guide you toward reaching your goals and sustaining them with resilience and clarity.

A Winning Mindset

Week 14

THINK DIFFERENTLY: THE CATALYST FOR YOUR RADICAL SUCCESS JOURNEY

"The definition of insanity is doing the same thing over and over and expecting a different result." You've heard it, I've heard it, but how often have we applied this age-old wisdom to our thinking patterns? The repetitive act of thinking the same way is a surefire route to boxing ourselves into a corner of stagnant results. At RAD Strategic Partners, we firmly believe that the way to rev up your success engine is to adopt a habit of thinking differently.

The Benefits of Divergent Thinking

Let's not just pontificate on the glory of different thought patterns. Instead, let's explore the tangible benefits that come along with it:

1. **Innovation and Inspiration:** Thinking differently invigorates us to break out of the conventional and embrace innovation. Businesses that think differently, such as Apple, Tesla, and Amazon, redefine markets and consumer behavior.
2. **Prevention of Groupthink:** Too much agreement can be detrimental to your success. Think Enron or the subprime mortgage crisis—instances where groupthink and excessive confidence led to disastrous outcomes.

3. **Risk-Taking and Change:** Risk aversion can kill progress. Individuals and companies who've revolutionized industries—from the Wright brothers to Elon Musk—have thought differently and taken risks.
4. **The Pursuit of Greatness:** Thinking outside of the proverbial box allows us to tap into untapped opportunities. It's this kind of thinking that shatters ceilings and rewrites history books.

Questions to Propel You Forward

How do you begin this journey to think differently? By asking yourself transformative questions, of course:

- **Skill Set Evaluation:** Are my skills as sharp as they could be? If not, it's high time you invest in upgrading them.
- **Winning Attitude:** Am I nurturing a positive mindset? Our Winning Attitude Quiz can help you gauge where you stand.
- **Career Choices:** Why am I in my current profession? Reflect on this to ensure it aligns with your life goals.
- **Past versus Future:** What old thoughts am I clinging to that don't serve my future?
- **Reality Check:** How much of what I "know" has been debunked? Stay updated.

Practical Tips for Thinking Differently

After asking yourself these pivotal questions, integrate the following practices into your daily life:

- **Eliminate Negative Thoughts:** Recognize and counteract your negative thinking with positive affirmations.
- **Be Inquisitive:** Adopt the habit of asking questions—of yourself and others. The more you inquire, the more you'll discover, and that's a rabbit hole worth diving into.

- **Play "What If":** Challenge yourself with hypothetical scenarios. This mental exercise can reveal unseen pathways and solutions.
- **Daydream:** Set aside time to let your mind wander towards your dreams. The simple act of daydreaming can fuel your subconscious to work towards turning those dreams into reality.
- **Solicit and Provide Feedback:** Don't shy away from post-mortems, whether things have gone spectacularly well or belly-up. Feedback loops are crucial for continuous improvement.

By adopting a mindset that actively seeks to think differently, you set yourself on a trajectory for unparalleled growth and, dare we say, RADical success. So, what are you waiting for?

Thinking differently opens up new possibilities and creative solutions, essential for overcoming challenges and driving innovation. To sustain this creative mindset, it's equally important to cultivate inner peace and clarity. Meditation provides a powerful tool to look within, helping us stay focused and centered amidst the hustle and bustle of daily life.

As we wrap up our exploration of thinking differently, it's clear that innovation and creativity often stem from a willingness to challenge conventional wisdom and view the world through a new lens. However, to truly unlock our creative potential, we must also turn our attention inward. Internal reflection through meditation allows us to quiet the noise of daily life, fostering a deeper connection with our inner thoughts and emotions. This introspective practice not only enhances our mental clarity but also serves as a wellspring for creative solutions and new perspectives. In the next section, we'll delve into the power of meditation and how looking within can inspire and sustain our ability to think differently.

Reroute to Success: Your Action Item Blueprint

So, you're mentally prepped and eager to ditch that conventional thinking, right? What's the first move? Here it is:

Action Item: Jot down one area where traditional thinking has been your stumbling block in the past six months. Next to it, list three "different" approaches to tackling this challenge. Pick one to implement over the next month.

Why this exercise? As we always say at RAD Strategic Partners, shifting your mindset is the foundational step for architecting your RADical success blueprint. By pinpointing the barriers and actively pursuing a new course of action, you're doing more than gathering insights— you're constructing a tactical plan for success.

> **"**
> Innovation distinguishes between a leader and a follower.
> **"**

Steve Jobs

Week 15

MEDITATE TO LOOK WITHIN: YOUR GATEWAY TO RADICAL SUCCESS

In the temple of Apollo, an ancient maxim says, "Know thyself." This profound wisdom holds the key to a journey filled with happiness, self-discovery, and RADical success. Understanding yourself—your passions, strengths, and weaknesses—translates into a life of fewer obstacles and greater joy. And guess what? The most successful people often embark on this journey through a powerful tool: meditation.

Insights from the Successful

So, why meditate? When you turn your gaze inward, clarity and innovation emerge. You uncover areas for growth and spots of pure joy. Making this introspection a habit sets you on a lifetime path of development, achievement, and RADical success. Meditation isn't just a practice; it's a rendezvous with your inner world, a space where external chaos fades and profound understanding arises.

Think it's just a fad? Legends like Jerry Seinfeld, Katy Perry, Bill Gates, Timothy Ferriss, RuPaul, and Michael Jordan might disagree. Their success stories often include meditation as a pivotal chapter. With endorsements like these and minimal opposition, meditation seems like a no-brainer.

The Diversity of Meditation: Finding Your Path

The beauty of meditation lies in its diversity. Whether through prayer, yoga, or simply listening to the waves, it's about finding your personal sanctuary. There's a plethora of advice on how to meditate—forms, durations, times of the day. Here's a RAD tip: start simple. Even one minute a day can set the foundation. I began with just a minute and now indulge in twenty to thirty minutes of meditation daily.

Advanced Meditation: Asking the Right Questions

As you master unplugging from the world and delving within, level up by integrating intention or reflective questions into your practice. Here are a few to kick-start your introspective journey:

- What is my definition of greatness?
- Where am I being lenient with myself?
- How boundless are my dreams?
- Do I often let "realistic" goals hinder my aspirations?
- Who is the "me" I aspire to become?
- Am I meeting my personal standards?

The frequency and honesty with which you confront these questions correlate directly with your success. Self-knowledge empowers you to steer your journey less swayed by external influences. I've witnessed clients who initially chased dreams molded by others, only to find authentic success when they pursued their true passions. Maximum success is achievable when you tread a path chosen through sincere introspection.

Deciding Who You Want to Be: The Path to RADical Success

Deciding who you want to be sets the stage for becoming that person. Dream without limits, and don't let the concept of "impossible" deter you. Remember, there was a time when going to the moon, accessing the internet, or having a portable phone seemed unattainable. Greatness emerges from conquering the impossible, not succumbing to the confines of reality.

The Transformative Impact of Meditation

Meditation not only calms the mind but also transforms it. Through this practice, you can reshape your thought patterns, cultivate a positive mindset, and open doors to creative solutions. It's about building resilience, enhancing focus, and fostering emotional stability. Meditation isn't just a journey inward; it's an evolution of the self.

Meditation in Daily Life: Integrating the Practice

Incorporating meditation into your daily routine need not be daunting. It can be as simple as taking a few moments of silence with your morning coffee, practicing mindful breathing during a break, or unwinding with a short meditation session before bed. The key is consistency and finding a rhythm that works for you. As it becomes a natural part of your day, you'll notice the subtle yet significant changes it brings to your life and work.

Embrace Meditation, Embrace Success

Meditation is more than a practice; it's a journey towards understanding and empowering yourself. By looking within, you discover your unique path to RADical success. So, take the leap, embrace meditation, and watch as it transforms your life, one mindful moment at a time.

Taking Action: Your First Step Towards a Mindful Journey

All right, you're inspired and ready to embrace meditation for RADical success. But what's the immediate next step? Here's a simple yet effective action item to kick-start your journey:

Action Item: Create Your Meditation Starter Kit

1. **Find Your Guide:** Read the book *Unplug* by Suze Yalof Schwartz and download the accompanying app.[9] These resources are fantastic tools to guide you on your meditation journey.
2. **Set Your Space:** Identify a quiet corner in your home or office where you can meditate without interruptions. It doesn't have to be elaborate—a comfortable chair or a cushion in a peaceful spot will do.
3. **Schedule Your Time:** Decide on a specific time each day for meditation. It could be early morning, during your lunch break, or before bedtime. Consistency is key.
4. **Start Small:** Begin with just a few minutes of meditation each day. Use the *Unplug* app to guide you through your first sessions.
5. **Track Your Progress:** Keep a journal or use an app to note your experiences, feelings, and any changes you observe.

Why are we doing this? As we say at RAD Strategic Partners, embarking on a journey of self-discovery is the foundation of achieving RADical success. By creating your meditation starter kit, you're not just flirting with the idea of mindfulness—you're equipping yourself with the tools to make it a reality. This is about transforming a concept into a daily practice. Ready, set, unplug!

---

[9] https://www.unplug.app/signup

Week 16

PRACTICE HAPPINESS: CULTIVATING POSITIVITY FOR RADICAL SUCCESS

Unlocking the Power of Positivity

Practicing happiness isn't just a feel-good mantra; it's a strategy with tangible benefits. Cultivating a positive mindset can lead to better performance, and teams that embrace positivity often see remarkable results. A substantial body of evidence directly links life satisfaction to business success. By choosing happiness, you're not just elevating your mood—you're building a stronger business and fostering a robust team.

Myth Busting: Happiness Beyond DNA and Circumstances

It's a common misconception that our happiness is dictated by our DNA or environment—that if we could just overcome one more hurdle, happiness and productivity would follow. However, research debunks this myth. Success is a moving target; it's about the pursuit rather than the achievement. By training ourselves to be positive, every measure of success improves.

Overcoming Challenges with a Positive Mindset

While depression, hormones, brain chemistry, and physical health play roles in our lives, we're not entirely at their mercy. Working towards positivity and happiness trains our bodies and brains to respond differently to challenges. This doesn't imply that happiness practitioners never feel down or experience sadness. We're human, after all. But this practice allows us to bounce back more quickly and mitigates the negative impact on our outcomes.

Three Simple Steps to Practice Happiness

1. **Choose Happiness Consciously** Every event or challenge presents an opportunity to view it positively. The room wasn't what you expected. Wow, look at that view! Life throws lemons? It's time to make lemonade. Remember, we control our responses.
2. **Practice New Habits** Evaluate and change destructive habits. Incorporate practices like gratitude, meditation, exercise, and journaling—all pathways to positive mindsets and increased happiness.
3. **Enjoy the Journey** Focus less on the destination, as goals constantly evolve. Appreciate each day without dwelling on the past or fearing the future. Find potential happiness in every moment.

Translating Happiness into Business and Team Success

Choosing positivity, practicing gratitude, and building solid connections are skills we can nurture within a business framework. From my retail days, I recall how warmly welcoming every customer and genuinely thanking them for every purchase kept our attitudes positive and cultivated a friendly, productive work environment.

Happy workplaces attract quality employees who generate real value for customers and foster business growth. People gravitate towards businesses that give them a good feeling and share their contagious positive attitudes. By implementing a happiness plan and sharing it with those around us, we create more opportunities for everyone.

Loving Life: The Ultimate Happiness

Taking inspiration from Mike Dooley, remember, "It's more important to love life than to be happy." When we learn to love life, we find happiness in every moment without actively pursuing it. Loving life involves engagement, nurturing, and growth—critical components of RADical success!

We can transform our approach to life and business by embracing these principles. Let's embark on this journey of practicing happiness together and witness the remarkable transformation it brings!

Choose Happiness

Turning Happiness into Action

You're inspired and ready to infuse happiness into your life and business. But what's the immediate next step? It's time for action.

Action Item: Reflect on a recent moment when you felt stressed or negative. Write it down. Next to it, jot down a positive perspective or lesson you could take from that situation. For example, if you faced a challenging client, the lesson might be improving communication or patience. Now, transform that lesson into a proactive goal for the next month. This could be, "I will practice active listening in all client meetings."

Why are we doing this? Remember, as we advocate at RAD Strategic Partners, embracing happiness is not just about feeling good; it's about transforming those feelings into tangible results. By identifying positive perspectives and setting actionable goals, you're not just embracing a happier outlook but translating it into a strategic plan for RADical success. Let's not just dream about happiness; practice it daily!

Week 17

DISCOVER THE MAGIC OF ZEN: UNLEASH YOUR INNER ZEN MASTER

The Weight of Judgment and Fear

The constant judgment and fear of failure that seem to accompany every decision and action in our lives can be exhausting, draining, and paralysis-causing. Do you wish there was a way to navigate the challenges of business and life without feeling overwhelmed or discouraged? Well, get ready to embrace the magic of Zen thinking and transform your perspective on success and happiness.

The Zen Farmer's Wisdom

The story of the Taoist Zen farmer is a fascinating tale that holds valuable lessons for all of us. It's time to dive into the world of Zen and unlock its incredible power to revolutionize how we approach our goals, relationships, and ultimately, our lives. Get ready to embark on a humorous and entertaining journey filled with laughter, enlightenment, and a sprinkle of ideas to catapult your success.

What is Zen Thinking?

So, what exactly is Zen thinking? It's a mindset that transcends the boundaries of right and wrong, good and bad. Imagine a world where our actions are not judged but seen as steps toward our desired outcome. It's a world where conversations become less challenging, problems become less catastrophic, and our ability to see the necessary steps expands. In this realm, there are no negative actions—only actions that didn't quite bring the imagined result. Or hey, maybe they did, depending on how we imagined it!

The Trap of Self-Judgment

Most of us operate with more judgment than we realize. It's true! Whenever something doesn't go our way, we tend to label it as "wrong" or "terrible." We even go as far as imagining what others might be thinking and judging ourselves based on those assumptions. The same is true in reverse. But what if I told you that this constant self-judgment blinds us to the steps and opportunities right before us? It's time to break free from this cycle of self-doubt and embrace the wonders of Zen.

Five Steps to Kick-Start Your Zen Journey

Now, let's put this practice into action. Here are five steps to kick-start our Zen journey:

1. **Watch the Story of the Zen Farmer:** Immerse yourself in the wisdom of the Zen farmer. This timeless tale reminds us that we can never predict the future or the path that events will lead us on.[10]
2. **Reflect on Events as Neutral Occurrences:** Reflect on the events of your day without labeling them as good or bad. Focus on how you can improve next time.
3. **Analyze Satisfying vs. Unsatisfying Events:** Dive deep into what truly brings you joy and fulfillment. Approach each experience without prejudgment.
4. **Repeat Daily:** Engage in daily sessions of embracing the Zen mindset. Consistency is key to making it our default mode of thinking.

---

[10] https://youtu.be/PM5TfT6mPU8

5. **Embrace the Power of Action:** When things don't go as expected, focus on taking action rather than judging the moment.

Embrace the Magic of Zen By embracing the Zen mindset, we can gain clarity, focus, and objectivity in every situation. It allows us to see beyond the short-term results and focus on our long-term vision. Remember, our choices are just that—choices. They are not inherently good or bad, right or wrong. They simply are. So, why not embrace this magical formula that brings objectivity, clarity, satisfaction, and joy into our lives?

It's time to release the judgment, fear, and self-doubt that have been holding us back. Embrace the magic of Zen and witness the transformation it can bring to our business, relationships, and overall well-being. Give it a try, and let the enchantment of Zen guide us on a path toward RADical success and fulfillment. Remember, there's no right or wrong, only the power of choice and the beauty of the present moment.

Zen in Action: Transforming Setbacks into Stepping Stones

You're ready to embrace the Zen mindset, but how do you make the first move? Don't worry; we've got a simple yet effective action item for you.

Action Item: Find a quiet spot and take a deep breath. Reflect on a recent event or situation that didn't go as planned. Without any judgment, simply describe it as a neutral occurrence. Now, identify one positive perspective or opportunity this event might have opened up, even if it's not immediately apparent. It could be a lesson learned, a new connection, or even the realization that you're more resilient than you thought.

Why are we doing this? Well, as we say at RAD Strategic Partners, recognizing the neutrality of events is the key to unlocking your Zen potential. By shifting your perspective from judgment to opportunity, you're not just coping with life's curveballs but transforming them into stepping stones towards your RADical success. This exercise helps you practice the art of seeing beyond immediate judgments and finding the hidden gems in every situation.

Month 5

BUILD SUCCESS HABITS

Habit Heroes: Constructing the Cornerstones of RADical Success

Welcome to the blueprint for building habits that aren't just good—they're transformative. This section is about embedding practices into your daily life that aren't just about doing but about being. It's where we fine-tune the inner mechanisms that drive outer success.

We begin with the practice of unplugging to recharge and then move on to the simple yet profound power of kindness. It's like a boomerang: throw it out into the world and watch it return, often when you least expect it. Next, it's all about focusing on your strengths. Like a master craftsman, you'll learn to hone your skills to perfection.

Faith in ourselves and the world around us is our next cornerstone. It's not just about believing; it's about knowing deep down that we're part of something bigger and that the universe conspires in our favor.

Finally, we dial up our creativity. In a world where thinking outside the box is often the key to unlocking success, you'll learn to turn your imagination into your most valuable asset.

Are you ready to cultivate these habit heroes? They're the silent guardians of your RADical success journey, steadily steering you towards your vision of achievement and fulfillment. Let's build them one empowering habit at a time.

Week 18

UNPLUG AND RECHARGE: REVITALIZE YOUR ENERGY AND FOCUS

The Plight of Modern Burnout

Do you sometimes feel like your batteries need a recharge? Are you running on empty, wiped out every day and every week? Burnout is the number one cause of business failure. It leads to a lack of focus and fulfillment, making even the simplest tasks appear insurmountable.

A Lesson from Our Ancestors

The cave dwellers spent their days hunting, gathering, napping, and being chased by tigers. That worked for them because there was a balance to their days, which gave them enough energy to outrun the tiger. We spend far too much time running from the tigers in modern society, which depletes our energy! Spending most of our time with our adrenaline pumping isn't healthy. We need both the adrenaline rush and rest periods in between to continue to function at an optimal level.

The Irony of Modern Connectivity

A meme floating around the internet says, "When the phone was tied with wire, humans were free." That statement resonates more each day. Those old enough to remember the days before mobile phones remember when we could turn them off anytime we wanted.

No one panicked if we didn't return a text or email in an hour, and it was possible to spend time in nature, free from interruption. Today, people expect us to be always on and available unless we train those around us differently. (More on that in another chapter). It is becoming increasingly difficult to turn off and unplug.

The Importance of Unplugging

The harder it becomes to unplug, the more vital it becomes that we do it. Want to increase your productivity, creativity, and energy? Try turning the devices off for a day, a weekend, or a vacation, and see what a reset can do. Ideally, we should unplug for at least one day each week, one weekend each quarter, and one vacation each year. The more we recharge our batteries, the better the results!

Strategies for Unplugging

How do we unplug so we can recharge?

1. **Disconnect from Devices:** Turn off the phone. Leave a message saying you are unavailable. Some people will leave a message, and others will reach out again after your return. We reduce stress by letting people know when to expect our return call.

2. **Ignore Other Digital Distractions:** Leave the other devices alone. Our email can wait. Leave an out-of-office reply. Yes, we might have tons of emails when we return, but much of that can be deleted when we only deal with messages requiring an action or reply. Taking the time to organize and create rules for our emails makes this much more manageable when done ahead of time.

3. **Shun the News and Entertainment:** Get rid of the remote control, the social feed, and the newspaper delivery. Trust me; nothing in the news can't wait a few days. I have vacationed for many years, detached from world events, and found that whenever a truly catastrophic event occurred, someone told me about it.

4. **Embrace Timelessness:** Finally, take off the watch, unplug the clocks, sit back, and enjoy.

Utilizing Free Time Wisely

What can we do with all this time? Spend it with friends and family. Read a book or magazine. Lie in the sun. Play with our kids. Take a nap. Keep a journal. Work on a hobby. It doesn't matter; it's just about recharging.

The Power of Unplugging

When we take some time to stop the constant demands for our time and attention through the devices we carry, we reset our brains, nervous systems, and thought patterns. We can't operate at our best when we constantly run without ever stopping to recharge, just like our phones. Make it a practice to unplug regularly to create RADical success.

Unplug

Unplugged Actions: Making the Most of Your Recharge Time

Now that you understand the importance of unplugging, what's your immediate next step? Here's a simple yet impactful action:

Action Item: Plan a day for a digital detox. Pick a date within the next month when you will turn off all your devices for at least twenty-four hours. Write it down in your calendar.

Why are we doing this? At RAD Strategic Partners, we believe that unplugging is a crucial step toward achieving RADical success. By committing to this digital detox, you're not just giving yourself a break but setting the stage for enhanced creativity, productivity, and well-being. It's not just about taking a break; it's about rejuvenating your mind and spirit to come back stronger.

Week 19

UNLEASH THE POWER OF KINDNESS: BUILD CONNECTIONS THROUGH COMPASSION

"No act of kindness, no matter how small, is ever wasted."
- Aesop

The Irrefutable Power of Kindness

Countless studies, including those from the Mayo Clinic,[11] point to one undeniable truth: kindness has profound benefits. Think of it as your mental and emotional Swiss Army knife. It boosts self-esteem, cuts down stress, and turbocharges productivity. And the best part? Kindness is as contagious as a hit summer tune.

Why Kindness Matters in Every Sphere

In life as in business, we don't just tolerate kindness; we're drawn to it like a magnet. Companies that consistently show compassion aren't merely accumulating customers; they're creating an army of raving fans. Kindness in the workplace doesn't just fill the room with

---

[11] https://connect.mayoclinic.org/blog/living-with-mild-cognitive-impairment-mci/newsfeed-post/the-power-of-kindness/

positive vibes; it's the secret sauce for unprecedented collaboration and innovation.

Customer Loyalty: A Case Study

Take, for example, the FedEx guy who goes the extra mile to deliver my packages or American Express sending out unexpected gifts. These seemingly small acts build a reservoir of loyalty that is priceless in today's competitive marketplace.

Do You Cultivate Kindness?

Now, ask yourself: are you merely a passive participant in this world of kindness, or are you an active contributor? You don't need to make grand gestures. Sometimes a warm smile or a simple "thank you" can transform someone's day, and, miraculously, make that cranky neighbor someone you'd genuinely invite to your family BBQ.

The Domino Effect of Kindness

When you practice intentional kindness, you don't just improve your immediate environment—you spark a chain reaction. A kindness-filled interaction can turn a one-time customer into a lifelong advocate or transform a disengaged team member into an enthusiastic collaborator.

Three Pillars for Building a Kindness Culture

1. **Intentional Acts:** The choices we make define us. Whether it's sending handwritten notes, recognizing milestones, or even offering a listening ear, our intentional acts of kindness send a powerful message.
2. **Subconscious Signals:** Every second, we are sending out subconscious signals to the world. From the clothes we wear to the tone we use, we're telling people who we are.

If you're dressed like you care and speak with kindness, that's more than half the battle won in the eyes of your stakeholders.

3. **The Attitude Factor:** Attitude isn't just a mindset; it's a life choice. A kind disposition doesn't merely enrich your personal life; it can be the lynchpin of customer retention and employee satisfaction in your business.

The Science of Kindness

Kindness isn't just a moral virtue; it's neuroscience gold. Acts of kindness activate serotonin and dopamine—neurotransmitters responsible for feelings of satisfaction and well-being. So, when you practice kindness, you're not just earning social brownie points; you're investing in your neurological wellness.

The Bottom Line

To sum it up, kindness is a game changer. By committing to a culture of kindness, we not only make the world a better place, but we set ourselves and our businesses up for RADical success. So, why not start today? After all, the road to RADical success is a marathon, not a sprint. And what better way to make the journey meaningful than to sprinkle it with acts of kindness?

Time to Act: Your Immediate Step to Cultivate Kindness

So, you're inspired and fully committed to integrating kindness into your daily routine, both personally and professionally. But how do you make the first move? Let's make it straightforward.

Action Item: Perform three acts of kindness today. Take a moment to write down three small acts of kindness you can perform today. They can be as simple as paying for someone's coffee in line or giving a colleague a genuine compliment. Next to each act, write down a time you'll complete it by.

Why focus on immediate action? At RAD Strategic Partners, we believe that change begins with a single step. Committing to kindness is a powerful way to fuel your RADical success journey. These small acts aren't just gestures; they're your stepping stones toward building a culture of kindness—in life and in business. By noting these actions and setting a time frame, you transform abstract intent into concrete plans.

Week 20

EMBRACE YOUR UNIQUE STRENGTHS: LEVERAGING YOUR TALENTS FOR RADICAL SUCCESS

As business leaders and entrepreneurs, we often fall into the trap of believing we must become masters of all trades to lead with authority and effectiveness. We may think excelling in every facet of business is a requisite, but this pursuit often leads to mediocrity and burnout. Instead, the key is to focus on our unique strengths.

The Power of Complementary Teams

Rather than striving for personal proficiency in everything, we should concentrate on identifying and developing our strengths and then build a team that complements those. Seek out individuals who excel where we may falter, valuing diverse skills and perspectives that foster innovation and create a robust, well-rounded team.

A Harmonious Business Symphony

Consider a band where you are the lead guitarist. Your strength is mesmerizing with melodies. If you tried to be the drummer, bassist, and vocalist simultaneously, it would result in chaos. But with a skilled drummer, bassist, and vocalist, each member's strength is amplified, leading to a harmonious and memorable performance. Similarly, your business can achieve remarkable success when each team member focuses on their strengths and collaborates effectively.

Maximizing Potential through Recognition

By leveraging everyone's strengths, you maximize each person's potential and foster a supportive and positive work environment. People feel valued and appreciated for their talents, leading to higher satisfaction and loyalty.

Leading with Insight and Adaptability

Effective leadership and communication are crucial in building a team that thrives on diverse strengths. As a leader, you must understand each member's unique abilities and align their responsibilities accordingly. Encourage discussions about strengths and weaknesses and provide opportunities for collaborative learning and growth.

Spotlight on Successful Leaders

Reflecting on leaders like Oprah Winfrey, with her innate communicative abilities; Sheryl Sandberg, with her exceptional leadership and team-building prowess; and Richard Branson, who has continually leveraged his adventurous spirit, shows us the power of embracing and utilizing personal strengths.

A Call to Celebrate Our Strengths

Focusing on our strengths isn't about ignoring areas for improvement; it's about acknowledging that nurturing our natural talents and leveraging them effectively can lead to success. By understanding our signature strengths and assembling a team with complementary skills, we can create a synergy that elevates our business.

So, let's commit to focusing on what makes us and our teams exceptional, leading like a conductor, and getting ready for a business performance that resonates long after the curtain falls. Remember, by celebrating and optimizing our unique strengths, we're not just aiming for success—we're composing a legacy.

Taking Center Stage with Your Strengths

Now that we've hit the high note on embracing our strengths, you might be wondering how to translate this melody into action. Here are simple steps to begin your transformation.

Action Item: Identify Your Encore Strengths

- First, take a moment to reflect on your recent work or life experiences. Identify a project or challenge where you felt in tune and in control.
- Write down this encore strength—a skill or talent that felt as natural to you as breathing, something that you excel in and enjoy.
- Next to it, list ways you can amplify this strength in your current role or business. Are there tasks you can take on that will allow this strength to shine?
- Finally, commit to one action you will take this month to leverage this strength. It could be volunteering for a new project, teaching a skill to others, or simply allocating more time to areas where this strength can be utilized.

Why do this exercise? As the maestros at RAD Strategic Partners will tell you, hitting the right notes with our strengths isn't just about self-awareness—it's about orchestrating our actions to create a symphony of success. By pinpointing and playing to your strengths, you're not just preparing for a performance but setting the stage for a standing ovation in your career. Remember, every day presents a new stage for you to showcase your talents. Make it count by focusing on your Encore Strengths, and watch how your business composition turns into a masterpiece of success.

Week 21

HAVE FAITH:
STAY RESILIENT IN TURBULENT TIMES

"Faith is a refusal to panic."
- D. Martyn Lloyd-Jones

These words resonate even more profoundly in today's ever-changing world. We're constantly bombarded with news of disruptions, crises, and uncertainties. Panic often seems like a natural response but rarely produces productive outcomes.

Amidst the chaos, having faith becomes your guiding light. It's the belief that you can weather any storm, that your company can adapt and thrive, and that the world, despite its challenges, is fundamentally sound.

1. **Have Faith in Yourself** Have you ever considered that every "first" in your life was uncomfortable? Your first day of school, your first job, even those first wobbly steps as a toddler. Yet, you not only survived but thrived. Trust that you possess the competence and adaptability to navigate uncharted waters. It's about believing in your ability to overcome challenges, grow, and succeed.

2. **Have Faith in Your Company** If your company is agile, well-managed, and open to adaptation, it's likely to weather crises successfully. History is rife with examples of businesses thriving during adversity. Take Procter & Gamble during the Great Depression; their innovation and resilience propelled them to greater heights. Even in tumultuous times, opportunities abound for those who can spot them. Be creative, look for new prospects, and take action.

3. **Have Faith in the World** Humanity is interconnected, and our shared bonds are most evident during crises. People help one another in times of need. The Comprehensive Emergency Response Team (CERT) training exemplifies how individuals band together effectively. Trust that when you lend a helping hand, it'll be reciprocated when you require it. The world has a way of providing support when it's most needed.

However, be discerning about the sources of your trust. Verify information, especially on social media, and avoid misplaced confidence in governmental institutions, prioritizing individuals over institutions. Expect change and be open to new ways of doing things. Life's journey is full of surprises, and adaptation is a testament to our resilience.

How to Avoid Panic

When the first signs of panic emerge, recite this affirmation: "I always find the resources necessary to face any problem. I have the tools and skills I need to reach my wildest dreams. Obstacles add to the journey and help me discover new paths. I am strong, and I am powerful. I am unstoppable."

Having a well-structured plan is invaluable. Live with intention and belief in your ability to execute your life plan. For comprehensive guidance on creating such a plan, refer to the RADical Planning section of this book.

In conclusion, faith is not about unquestioning optimism but maintaining composure and clarity amidst chaos. By having faith in yourself, your company, and the world, you can rise above panic and make decisions that will lead to a brighter future. Trust in your resilience, adaptability, and the inherent goodness of humanity, and you'll find your path forward, even in the face of uncertainty.

Action Item: Cultivate Faith and Resilience

Now that you've embraced the power of faith and resilience, it's time to put it into action. Here's a simple yet impactful exercise to help you on your journey:

- **Reflect on Past Challenges:** Take a moment to think about a challenging situation you've faced in the past. It could be a personal or professional setback, a difficult decision, or a moment when you felt overwhelmed.
- **Identify Lessons Learned:** Next to this challenge, jot down at least one valuable lesson you learned. Consider how this lesson has contributed to your growth, even if it was a challenging experience.
- **Set a Proactive Goal:** Now, translate that lesson into a proactive goal for the upcoming month. This goal should reflect how you intend to apply your lesson. It could be a specific action, a change in mindset, or an opportunity you want to pursue based on your newfound wisdom.
- **Keep a Journal:** Throughout the month, maintain a journal to track your progress. Reflect on how your faith and resilience help you overcome new challenges and make better decisions.
- **Review and Adapt:** At the end of the month, review your progress and the insights you've gained. Adjust your goals and strategies as needed, and continue this practice to reinforce your faith and resilience.

By embracing this action item, you're not only stopping at insights, you're translating them into a tangible game plan for personal and professional growth. Remember, understanding and learning from challenges is the cornerstone of your journey to RADical success.

Week 22

INCREASE CREATIVITY AND INNOVATION: NINE PROVEN WAYS TO UNLOCK YOUR POTENTIAL

In today's fast-paced world, creativity and innovation are more than just buzzwords—they're the currency of success. Whether in business or life, the ability to innovate sets you apart from the rest. But what is the secret sauce to fostering creativity and innovation? Let's delve into nine actionable strategies that can turbocharge your creative juices and inspire those around you to be more innovative.

1. **Embrace Constant and Never-Ending Improvement** "The pursuit of excellence" should be your mantra. It's not about achieving perfection; it's about constantly striving to improve. Think of musicians, athletes, or entrepreneurs. They never stop honing their skills. From minor tweaks to paradigm shifts, continuous improvement is the cornerstone of innovation.

2. **Challenge Your Long-Held Beliefs** Times change, and so should you. Being wedded to old methods or beliefs can be the most significant obstacle to innovation. Whether it's sticking to obsolete technology or old-school ideologies, refusing to adapt can stifle your creativity. Open your mind to new perspectives and be willing to pivot.

3. **Read Widely and Wisely** Continuous learning fuels your creative engine. Books, articles, podcasts—consume them voraciously. The more knowledge you gain, the richer the soil in which new ideas can sprout. Try revisiting old resources with a fresh perspective; you'll be surprised at the gems you'll unearth.

4. **Diversify Your Social Circle** Spend time with people from diverse industries, cultural backgrounds, and financial standings. You'd be amazed at how varied perspectives can trigger "aha!" moments. According to a 2017 study reported on by the Harvard Business Review,[12] diversity can significantly enhance innovation.

5. **Question Everything** Analyze your actions critically. Are they yielding the results you desire? If not, it's time to change your approach. As we say at RAD Strategic Partners, "What got you here won't get you there." Don't let habits eclipse innovation.

6. **Eliminate the Fear of Failure** What would you do if you knew you couldn't fail? Fear of failure can be paralyzing, but remember, Thomas Edison had 1,000 unsuccessful attempts before inventing the light bulb. Celebrate failures as stepping stones towards your success.

7. **Collaborate for Creativity** Two heads are better than one. Indeed, a study from the Institute for Corporate Productivity [13] showed that collaborative work could boost performance and creativity. Use brainstorming sessions, engage with mentors, or join mastermind groups to flesh out those ground-breaking ideas.

---

[12] https://hbr.org/2017/03/teams-solve-problems-faster-when-theyre-more-cognitively-diverse

[13] https://www.forbes.com/sites/adigaskell/2017/06/22/new-study-finds-that-collaboration-drives-workplace-performance/?sh=1b47cd83d025

8. **Have Fun** The best ideas often come when you're relaxed and enjoying yourself. Inject fun into your activities to stimulate creativity and lower stress levels. After all, a joyful mind is an innovative mind.

9. **Promote Risk-Taking** Encourage your team, family, and yourself to step out of your comfort zone. Innovative thinking flourishes when we're open to taking calculated risks. It's about creating a culture where it's okay to fail but unacceptable not to try.

The Power of Creativity in Fueling Success

Creativity is not a solo act; it thrives within a community and shapes the future. By embracing these strategies, you set the stage for a culture of innovation that breeds RADical success. So, go ahead. Stir the pot, shake things up, and let your creativity run wild. Your RADical journey to innovation starts now.

Creativity Puzzle

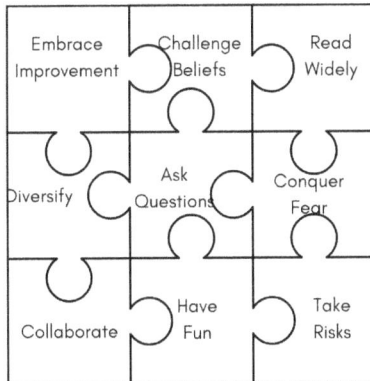

Embrace Improvement	Challenge Beliefs	Read Widely
Diversify	Ask Questions	Conquer Fear
Collaborate	Have Fun	Take Risks

Ready to Ignite Your Creative Spark? Here's Your Next Step

Now that you're buzzing with inspiration to be the creative dynamo you're meant to be, let's talk about putting this all into action.

Action Item: Jot down one area in your business or personal life where you feel your creativity or innovation has been lacking. Beside it, list three concrete steps you can take this month to ramp up your creative energies in that domain. Whether it's reading a specific book, engaging in a brainstorming session, or simply taking an afternoon off to recharge and get inspired—write it down.

Why are we doing this? You know how it goes at RAD Strategic Partners—ideas alone don't drive RADical success. Action does. By identifying your "creativity gaps" and setting actionable plans, you're moving beyond mere insights and creating a tangible strategy for your innovative journey.

And remember, action begets action. Today's creative spark is tomorrow's wildfire of innovation. Let's turn those sparks into flames, shall we?

Month 6

BECOME A LEADER

Elevating Leadership: Cultivating Your Command for RADical Success

Prepare to step into the role of the visionary, the guide, the trailblazer. This section is about more than leading—it's about embodying leadership in every gesture, decision, and strategy. It's time to build that leadership muscle and transform potential into palpable power.

Leadership is an art, a science, and a journey. We'll explore the mosaic of qualities that compose a great leader, the kind that inspires action, fosters innovation, and ignites change. You'll discover that authentic leadership isn't about authority—it's about authenticity, connection, and the willingness to grow alongside your team.

The final piece of the puzzle is developing your leadership mindset. This is where you shift from simply doing leadership to being a leader. It's a subtle but RADical shift that will permeate the essence of your personal and professional life, propelling you and those you lead toward a shared horizon of success.

By the end of this section, you'll understand what makes a great leader and be on your way to becoming one. Ready to command your destiny? Let's forge your leadership legacy.

Week 23

COMMIT TO LIFELONG GROWTH: THE EVERGREEN STRATEGY FOR RADICAL SUCCESS

In an ever-evolving world, the commitment to personal growth stands as the bedrock of sustained success in both life and business. At RAD Strategic Partners, we recognize that, much like the natural world, we either progress or regress; stasis is merely an illusion. Embracing this concept is not just beneficial—it's imperative for those seeking RADical success. But what does it mean to commit to personal growth, and how can you ensure that this commitment translates into tangible results?

The Nature of Growth

Growth is the underlying theme in every aspect of life, from nurturing a family to leading a company. However, it's easy to overlook personal development's most crucial growth. Like a tree stretching its branches towards the sun or slowly succumbing to decay, our businesses, relationships, and emotional skills follow a similar pattern. Ask yourself: What was the last enriching book you read? Which workshop did you last attend? These are the seeds of personal growth, and their cultivation is a deliberate choice.

The Roadmap to the Future

It's often said that our future state is determined by the books we read, the people we surround ourselves with, and our actions. This week, take a deliberate step by committing to a lifelong learning program—then take action to implement it.

Defining Personal Growth

We can understand personal growth as expanding one's skills, knowledge, and attributes. It's about setting and achieving life goals and enhancing one's outlook on life. This encompasses enriching behavior and habits and adopting techniques to establish positive routines, actions, and reactions.

Strategies for Personal Development

Once you commit, several strategies can kick-start your journey:

- **Immerse Yourself in Literature:** Whether you pick up a book written to boost business acumen, enhance leadership qualities, or simply inspire, reading is a fundamental step toward growth.
- **Engage in Seminars and Workshops:** Opportunities for learning from experts abound. Seek them out and engage actively.
- **Leverage Digital Media:** Purchase and actively engage with digital content that aligns with your growth goals. Remember, the actual value lies in application, not accumulation.
- **Stay Informed:** Subscribe to industry magazines, newsletters, or blogs. Stay current and apply new insights to keep your knowledge base fresh.
- **Take Local Classes:** Community colleges and local institutions offer a wealth of knowledge across various subjects. These new skills often translate into unexpected opportunities.

- **Adopt Success Habits:** Successful individuals often share standard practices such as exercising, reading, meditating, planning, and maintaining focus. Emulate these habits to align with their trajectory of success.

As a seasoned business coach, my commitment to continuous growth is non-negotiable. Daily reading, regular meditation, attending workshops, and participating in mastermind groups form the core of my growth strategy. What does your commitment look like?

Evaluating Time for Growth

If you struggle to find time for personal development, assess your current activities. Could the time spent on television or casual reading be reallocated to enriching pursuits? Lifelong learning equates to lifelong value.

Earn More by Learning More

The correlation between knowledge and earnings is undeniable. You set the stage for future earnings and opportunities by asking yourself what you're learning.

You've already taken the first step by choosing to read this book. Now, I challenge you to continue the momentum by solidifying your commitment to growth. Remember, at RAD Strategic Partners, we're your partner for RADical success—and that partnership begins with the promise of perpetual progress.

Action Steps for Lifelong Learning

You're now aware that growth is not just a concept but a continuous journey that contributes to RADical success. So, what's the first tangible step you can take on this path? Let's make it simple yet effective.

Action Item: Select one skill or area of knowledge you've wanted to improve or learn more about but haven't yet started.

- **Commit to a Learning Source:** Choose a specific book, seminar, online course, or workshop related to that skill or knowledge area.
- **Set a Date:** Mark on your calendar the date you will begin this learning experience.
- **Share Your Commitment:** Tell a friend, colleague, or mentor about your commitment, or, even better, invite them to join you on this learning adventure.
- **Reflect and Apply Takeaways:** After completing your chosen learning activity, take a moment to reflect. Write down three key takeaways and how you'll integrate them into your daily life or work.

Why is this step crucial? As we often say at RAD Strategic Partners, embarking on a journey of personal growth is akin to planting a garden of opportunity. By choosing a specific area to develop and setting clear actions, you're not merely hoping for change but cultivating it. This proactive approach transforms the seeds of learning into the fruits of achievement on your unique path to RADical success.

Remember, lifelong learning isn't just about collecting knowledge; it's about transforming it into actions that propel you forward. Start with this action item and watch how it blossoms into profound progress.

Week 24

PRACTICE RADICAL SELF-DISCIPLINE: MASTER YOURSELF FOR OUTSTANDING RESULTS

Do you possess the unwavering self-discipline required to conquer your goals? True self-discipline manifests in the ability to motivate oneself, even in the face of negative emotions, to advance toward one's objectives. Are you the kind of person who shows up each day, delivering your best efforts regardless of how you feel? Individuals with strong self-discipline possess willpower, persistence, and focus, employing these tools to consistently push forward in their pursuits.

Whether conscious of it or not, most of us grapple with self-discipline to some extent. How often do you find yourself procrastinating or avoiding tasks that you dislike or that make you uncomfortable? Can you stay on track even on challenging days? Are you able to persist when immediate results elude you? Remember, winners habitually embrace discomfort, while losers shy away from it. Make a conscious choice to be a winner by cultivating self-discipline.

In our lives, we exhibit tremendous commitment and discipline toward many tasks without even considering them. Consider habits like brushing our teeth, engaging in our weekly golf game, watching our favorite show, or checking our social media accounts. Now, imagine the transformative outcomes if you applied this level of commitment to the tasks necessary for your business and personal growth.

Five Steps to Effortless Commitment

1. **Commit Fully:** Make an unwavering decision to be committed to these activities. Be authentic with yourself. It's either we commit to doing what it takes or resign ourselves to not reaching our goals. If we struggle to do what's necessary, it's time to reevaluate our plans. Write down your commitment and share it with others. Find someone who can hold you accountable. It's easy to let ourselves off the hook mentally, but it's not as simple when someone else checks in.

2. **Eliminate Excuses:** Discard all excuses, explanations, and justifications that hinder your accomplishments. These distractions only serve to obstruct your progress. Adopt a "no excuses" mindset and take action, no matter what.

3. **Schedule Tasks:** Incorporate these tasks into your calendar and treat them with utmost respect. Allocate the time you need to complete things by intentionally creating space for them. Utilize a scheduling system that helps you adhere to your commitments.

4. **Set Time Limits:** Experiment with time-bound commitments. For example, decide to engage in a task for a week, a month, or a quarter. This approach works particularly well for jobs you know are necessary but don't enjoy. It also proves effective for activities you believe you should be doing but are unsure of their effectiveness. Committing for a limited time allows you to dip your toes in the water and assess the results.

5. **Evaluate the Results:** Imagine if you dedicated yourself to these commitments every day for a month. What kind of results would you achieve? Could that motivate you to continue? Positive reinforcement works wonders in establishing positive habits.

By prioritizing self-discipline, you'll witness the results firsthand. It doesn't take long to observe positive outcomes. Developing these skills will allow you to make better use of your time and expand your available hours. Most people would agree that self-discipline is the ultimate path to success.

In conclusion, the path to success lies in practicing RADical self-discipline. Embrace the challenges, commit unwaveringly, eliminate excuses, schedule tasks, set time limits, and evaluate the results. Adopting these principles will cultivate the self-discipline necessary to achieve extraordinary results. Remember, self-discipline is not an arduous process but rather a transformative journey. Start today and witness its incredible impact on your life.

Action Item: RADical Self-Discipline Roadmap

Open that trusty note-taking app of yours and let's get down to brass tacks.

- **Commitment Contract:** Draft a letter of commitment to yourself, outlining your resolve to engage in the activities that align with your goals. Share this document with a trusted accountability partner. Don't go easy on yourself; you're the CEO of your own destiny.
- **Excuse Eraser:** Make a list of frequent excuses you find yourself using. For each excuse, jot down a counterargument that nullifies it. Whenever an excuse pops up, refer to your excuse-eraser list and proceed to take action.
- **Sacred Scheduling:** Go to your digital calendar right now and block off time for these vital tasks. Label these blocks as non-negotiables to amp up their priority status. Yes, this is your calendar doubling as a to-do list.
- **Time-Capsule Tasks:** Pick a task you've been dodging and commit to it for a limited time frame—say a month. Document your experience and results. This is your experiment lab, so put on your safety goggles.
- **Result Reflection:** After a month of disciplined action, assess the outcomes. What worked? What needs tweaking? Let the positive results serve as your motivational nudge for the next phase.

By actioning these steps, you're not just setting the table for success; you're basically inviting it to move in. At RAD Strategic Partners, we believe that self-discipline isn't a chore, it's a choice—a RADically empowering one at that.

Week 25

CULTIVATE THE QUALITIES OF A GREAT LEADER: EMPOWER AND INSPIRE TO DRIVE RADICAL SUCCESS

Leadership transcends the realm of buzzwords—it embodies a journey, a steadfast commitment, and a lifestyle dedicated to elevating those around us. It is a multifaceted art that intertwines the power of empowerment, the acumen of strategic collaboration, and the essence of realizing ambitious goals. Echoing Napoleon Hill's sentiments, leadership is undeniably a cornerstone skill for success.

At RAD Strategic Partners, we champion the notion that leadership is accessible to everyone. Irrespective of our current positions, there is room for growth and a chance to ascend as more influential visionaries. By fostering these five cardinal leadership traits, we set the stage for unprecedented achievements.

1. **Humility: The Silent Strength** Humility is the silent anthem of the greats—where actions resonate louder than any proclamations of self-worth. Humble leaders do not

diminish their lights; instead, they acknowledge their contributions and amplify the brilliance of their team. This self-awareness and willingness to share success define and refine a leader's humility. It's about doing extraordinary things and valuing the collaborative spirit.

2. **Passion: The Undeniable Spark** Passion, often unseen, is the relentless force propelling us toward our ambitions. The fervor ignites our dedication and magnetizes others to our cause. Rekindling this intrinsic flame is crucial to fostering a culture of enthusiasm and unwavering commitment.

3. **Integrity: The Trust Quotient** The currency of leadership is integrity. Living a life of honesty sets the foundation for trust, which is essential in all facets of leadership. It's a binary choice, with each action and decision contributing to a legacy of reliability. Bolstering integrity requires holding a mirror to our shortcomings and pledging to be unwaveringly honest.

4. **Responsibility: The Accountability Principle** Leadership is synonymous with accountability. This means facing challenges head-on and adopting the lessons learned to carve the pathway to growth. Pursuing excellence is relentless, and the leader's role is to nurture this ethos within their realm, turning feedback into the seeds of progress.

5. **Vision: Charting the Uncharted** Vision is the leader's telescope to the future. It represents the audacity to dream and the resolve to manifest those dreams into tangible realities. Visionaries are architects of the unseen, constructing bridges to possibilities and inviting others to cross them.

The Impact of Strong Leadership

The resonance of effective leadership is far-reaching, casting a luminescence on the pathway to success. As leaders, we become the lighthouse for aspiration, aligning with those who share our vision and moving together toward a common zenith. Leadership is not esoteric—it is the essence of tangible, attainable, and RADical success.

Leadership Effect on Results

Building upon these leadership qualities requires conscious effort and an environment conducive to growth. Incorporating real-world data, a study by the Center for Creative Leadership found that leaders who exhibit high levels of integrity and responsibility foster a culture of trust and high performance within their organizations.[14]

Moreover, a study found in Harvard Business Review underscores the significance of vision, demonstrating that leaders with a clear, engaging, and dynamic vision can propel their organizations up to twelve times higher in terms of financial performance than those without it.[15]

In cultivating our leadership garden, we must tend to these traits with the same dedication as a master gardener—nurturing, pruning, and providing the right environment for each to flourish.

Actionable Steps for Aspiring Leaders

1. **Reflect on Your Path to Humility:** Share a recent success story and the collaborative efforts behind it.
2. **Reignite Your Passion:** Identify and engage in an activity that reconnects you with your core motivations.
3. **Exercise Integrity:** Commit to complete transparency in your next team project.

---

[14] https://cclinnovation.org/the-irony-of-integrity-a-study-of-the-character-strengths-of-leaders/
[15] https://hbr.org/2009/01/to-lead-create-a-shared-vision

4. **Embrace Responsibility:** Select a recent challenge and analyze how you can own the outcome more effectively.
5. **Craft Your Vision:** Dedicate time to articulate your future goals and share them with your peers for feedback.

The path to RADical success is paved with personal growth and leadership development milestones. As we enhance these qualities within ourselves, we rise as individuals and lift our entire team towards a collective triumph.

Action Item: Strengthen Your Leadership Traits

Develop your leadership traits. Choose one leadership trait you want to focus on this week. Here's how to forge it into your routine:

- **For Humility:** Identify someone in your team who has been instrumental in a recent success. Craft a thoughtful acknowledgment (public or private) highlighting their contribution.
- **For Passion:** Take a moment to write down what aspect of your work excites you the most. Plan a small project or initiative that channels this passion, and observe its impact on your team's engagement.
- **For Integrity:** Reflect on a decision you've made in the past where you could've been more transparent. Commit to an action that will rectify this and strengthen trust with your colleagues.
- **For Responsibility:** Consider a recent situation where you could've taken more ownership. Write down three ways you will take responsibility in a similar future scenario.
- **For Vision:** Dedicate thirty minutes to draft a vision statement for your next big goal. Share it with a mentor or colleague for feedback, and commit to one step to bring you closer to that vision.

Why this exercise? At RAD Strategic Partners, we believe leadership skills are like muscles—the more you exercise them, the stronger they become. By actively integrating these traits into your daily life, you're not just aspiring to be a better leader—you're actively sculpting yourself into one. Each step you take is a building block in your journey of leading with distinction and achieving RADical success.

Week 26

MASTER THE LEADERSHIP MINDSET: UNLOCKING YOUR POTENTIAL AS A MANAGER

Embarking on the journey to become a more impactful leader is a transformation that starts within. The quest often centers around critical questions for business owners and executives: How do I refine my leadership capabilities? What makes a truly effective manager? How can I inspire peak performance in my team?

Adopt the Mindset for Mastery

It all begins with cultivating the right leadership mindset—a blend of psychology, emotional intelligence, and strategic thinking. The field of neuro-linguistic programming (NLP), renowned for its approach to communication and personal development, presents a robust framework for building this mindset.[16]

Ten NLP Presuppositions for Aspiring Leaders

1. **Perception vs. Reality:** Understand that your view of the world is not the whole truth. Leaders must acknowledge the diversity of perspectives in their teams.

---

[16] For more information on NLP: https://www.nlp.com/

2. **Patterns of Excellence:** Habits define our capabilities. To change outcomes, change your thought patterns.

3. **Modeling Success:** If one person can excel at a task, it can be replicated. Influential leaders mentor and coach their teams to replicate success.

4. **Mind–Body Connection:** Your mental state directly influences your behavior. Leaders can foster a culture of positivity and drive.

5. **Innate Resources:** Every person has untapped potential. It's a leader's job to recognize and cultivate this potential for the betterment of the individual and the organization.

6. **Constant Communication:** Every action communicates a message. Ensure your communication is intentional and clear.

7. **Responsive Communication:** If the response to your communication isn't what you expected, change your approach. The onus is on you as a leader to be understood.

8. **Positive Intent:** Every action has a positive intention. Understanding this can transform your response to team behaviors.

9. **Choice in Context:** People make the best choice they perceive. Provide your team with better options and watch their decision-making evolve.

10. **Adaptive Strategies:** If one approach fails, try another. Leaders must be agile and willing to experiment with new methods.

Cultivating a Leadership Garden

Embracing these principles can revolutionize your leadership style. It's akin to tending a garden—cultivate the soil (mindset), plant the seeds (principles), and nurture the growth (constant application and improvement).

The Manager's Mantra: Change Begins with Me

Leaders who invest in developing their mindset see the benefits multiply. They create environments where creativity thrives, solutions are plentiful, and teams genuinely engage.

Take the Lead: Embrace the Leadership Mindset

The leadership mindset isn't just an idea; it's a catalyst for transformation. As you internalize and live out these tenets, you lay the groundwork for incremental improvements and RADical success. The journey of a remarkable leader begins with a single yet powerful shift in perspective. Embrace this leadership mindset and watch as it shapes a promising path for you and your team.

> **"**
> Leaders don't force
> people to follow—they
> invite them on a journey.
> **"**

Charles S. Lauer

Transform Insight into Impact: Your Leadership Mindset Action Step

You're now familiar with the transformative power of the leadership mindset. But how do you translate this newfound knowledge into practical, everyday actions? Here's how you start:

Action Item: Map Your Mindset Shift

1. **Identify a Perception:** Choose one perception or preconceived notion you have about your team or management style.
2. **Challenge the Status Quo:** Write down how this perception has influenced your leadership approach so far.
3. **Seek the Reality:** Engage in a conversation with a team member to understand their perspective on this notion.
4. **Reshape Thinking:** Based on this dialogue, jot down new insights or an alternative understanding you've gained.
5. **Implement a Change:** Translate this insight into a specific, measurable action you will take over the next week to shift your approach.

Why is this exercise crucial? At RAD Strategic Partners, we recognize leadership growth stems from continuous self-reflection and the willingness to embrace alternative perspectives. This exercise is not merely about reflection—it's about actively reshaping your leadership landscape to foster a more inclusive, dynamic, and empowered team environment. Begin this practice, and you're setting the stage for a journey of RADical growth and success—for you and your team.

Month 7

BUILD A TEAM

The Power Circle: Rallying the Dream Team for RADical Success

Behind every great leader is a formidable cadre of allies, mentors, and champions. This section is dedicated to the people—the dream weavers—who will help turn your vision into reality. It's about recognizing that no one achieves greatness in a vacuum.

We'll identify the seven key people you need in your corner. From the mentor who shares wisdom to the coach who infuses your journey with enthusiasm, each plays a vital role in your narrative of success.

Surrounding yourself with supportive people isn't just a feel-good mantra; it's a strategic move. Like a gardener who carefully selects plants that thrive together, you'll learn to cultivate a network that uplifts and propels everyone toward collective success.

Building a tribe goes beyond networking—it's about fostering a community that shares your passion and drive. And let's not forget the importance of rewarding your team. Recognition is the fuel that keeps the engine of motivation running smoothly.

Prepare to harness the power of your circle. By the end of this section, you'll know whom you need by your side and how to create and nurture these connections for RADical success. Shall we begin the assembly of your champions?

Week 27

BUILD YOUR DREAM TEAM: SEVEN KEY PLAYERS YOU NEED IN YOUR CORNER

Embrace Team Synergy for Ultimate Success

It's a common misconception that success is a solo journey. The reality? It takes a village—or rather, a dream team—to truly excel in both your career and personal life. Valuing your time means investing it in the right people. Let's break down the essential roles for a team that will catapult you to RADical success.

1. **The Honest Friend** Honest friends are your unfiltered mirrors, your reality checks. They're the ones who aren't afraid to serve you the hard truths, keeping you accountable and authentically grounded. Treasure their candor— it's a compass that will guide you towards genuine self-improvement.

2. **The Connector** In the symphony of success, connectors are the conductors, the networking maestros. They're adept at weaving networks across various industries, introducing you to potential clients, partners, and a plethora of opportunities to help your business flourish.

3. **The Calm in the Storm** When the going gets tough, team members who serve as the calm in the storm are your anchors

amidst turbulence, your beacons of tranquility. Their poise under pressure isn't just reassuring, it's a powerful force that helps you maintain your focus and find clarity in chaos.

4. **The Tech Wizard** Tech Wizards are your innovators of the digital age, your key to staying ahead in a tech-driven world. They're the early adopters, the digital trendsetters who ensure that you're harnessing the full potential of modern technology to streamline your processes and edge out the competition.

5. **The Mentor** Mentors are not just advisors—they're your career's sages of success. With their experience, they illuminate paths you might have missed and challenge you to broaden your horizon, pushing you beyond the boundaries of your comfort zone.

6. **The Protégé** The journey of teaching is also one of learning. Protégés benefit from your guidance and offer fresh insights and a mirror to reflect on your journey. In nurturing their growth, you inadvertently polish your own leadership prowess.

7. **The Coach** Coaches are the catalyst for your growth. They're the strategists behind your victories, helping you identify your innate strengths and the areas you can fortify. Through their guidance, you'll journey towards becoming the best version of yourself.

Assembling Your A-Team

Building a robust support system is a deliberate process. It's about curating a team that complements your strengths and compensates for your vulnerabilities. With the right mix of individuals, there's no limit to what you can achieve. So, take stock of your current squad, pinpoint where you lack expertise, and actively seek out those who can fill those voids. Remember, a strong team thrives on reciprocity. Be ready to lend your expertise as well.

In conclusion, the essence of building a dream team lies in recognizing that every role is pivotal. By aligning with individuals who bring diverse strengths to the table, you set the stage for a symphony of success that resonates far beyond individual capabilities. It's time to rally your champions and embark on a journey to RADical success together.

Building your dream team lays the groundwork for collaborative success and innovation. With a strong team in place, the next step is to create an environment that naturally attracts success. By fostering a positive and opportunity-rich atmosphere, we can draw in the resources and opportunities needed to elevate our ventures to new heights

Action Steps: Assemble Your Dream Team

Now that you're fired up about constructing your all-star team, it's time to roll up your sleeves and draft your dream team roster. Let's break it down into actionable steps:

Action Item: Identify Your Team Gaps

1. Reflect on your current professional and personal support system. Where are the gaps? Do you have an honest friend, a connector, or a calm in the storm?
2. Write down the roles you lack and the ideal characteristics of individuals you need to fill these positions.

Action Item: Cultivate Connections

1. Next to each role, list at least one action you can take this month to connect with someone who embodies these traits. This could be attending a networking event, contacting a mentor, or signing up for a tech workshop.
2. Set specific goals for yourself. For example, "By the end of this month, I will have coffee with a potential mentor to discuss my business vision."

Why take these steps? Just as we affirm at RAD Strategic Partners, crafting your support network is like curating a gallery of greatness. By consciously identifying where you need support and proactively seeking out those individuals, you're not just dreaming of success—you're architecting it. So, what's your next move? Draft that email, make that call, and start turning those empty slots into a league of extraordinary collaborators.

Remember, every championship team was built one player at a time. Yours is no different. Let's start scouting for talent and building your dream team today.

Week 28

ATTRACT SUCCESS: SURROUND YOURSELF WITH THE PEOPLE YOU NEED

Understanding Your Influence

I was hanging out with a client, probably on one of our spa weekends, to do her annual business plan when her cell phone rang at an odd hour. "Why do people call me at such weird times?" she questioned. "Probably because you advertise twenty-four-hour availability!" I replied. And then we just cracked up. We are in control of whom we attract to our businesses and our lives. Sometimes we don't like to admit it.

Attracting the Right People

Are we attracting the people we want and need? Do we enjoy and benefit from the people in our lives, and do they bring out our best side, challenge us to improve, and support our dreams and goals? RADical success occurs when we actively surround ourselves with the people we desire.

Attracting the right people into our lives and businesses is essential to success. Whether we are looking for a new customer, business opportunity, team member, or friend, the people we surround ourselves with profoundly impact our growth and development.

Developing a method is far more effective than randomly stabbing at the marketplace, throwing darts at the resumes on Indeed, or approaching strangers on the street. Therefore, it is essential to have a method for attracting the ideal people into our lives and businesses.

Process for Attracting Those We Desire

1. **Write It Down**: Write down what we want and whom we are looking to attract. We need to take the time to answer a few questions to set our RAS (see chapter 41 for an explanation of the Reticular Activating System, or RAS) to focus on finding those people. Who is our ideal customer? What qualities make the perfect team member? Who are the people with whom we want to associate and grow? The more detailed we are, the easier it is to find them.

2. **Advertise Your Needs**: Once we have clarity on whom we want to meet, we need to tell people about it. We can ensure everyone in our sphere of influence knows whom we want to meet. The easiest way to do this is to tell them. Whether we are looking for a new client, business opportunity, team member, or friend, the more people we enlist in our search, the greater our chance of success.

3. **Show Up and Engage**: We need to find out where to interact with people who fit our description of the people we want to meet. We spend a lot of time with the people we regularly interact with, and relationships build from interactions. The best way to meet new people is to interact with new people. It can seem obvious, but it doesn't happen unless we take action.

4. **Consult the Mirror**: Finally, we need to look at ourselves and our businesses and ensure we present ourselves and our business in a fashion that would attract those people. Relationships are two-way streets, and we need to walk our part to attract others. It is essential to evaluate our values, goals, and vision to ensure we project an image that aligns with the people we want to attract.

Growing Your Circle

Clarity is critical to finding the people we need in our network. Once we are clear on whom we want to meet, and our actions align with that, it's easy to attract the right people for us. "Our people" are the big tribe of humans who contribute to our human experience and well-being. Our family, friends, business associates, networking partners, vendors, customers, peers, and many more support, enrich, and influence our lives. When we actively create a tribe aligned with our vision and goals, more happens with less effort, and our dreams come true.

However, attracting the right people into our lives is not always easy. It requires patience, persistence, and a positive mindset. We need to be willing to take risks, try new things, and step outside our comfort zone. We need to be open to new experiences and new people.

Moreover, it is important to understand that not everyone will fit into our network. We need to be willing to let go of the people who do not align with our values, vision, and goals. It can be challenging to let go of people, especially if we have a long history with them. However, it is necessary to surround ourselves with people who will support, challenge, and inspire us to be our best selves.

In addition to attracting the right people, being the right person is essential. We must continually work on ourselves, developing our skills, knowledge, and character. We need to be kind, empathetic, and supportive of others and be willing to listen, learn, and grow. We attract the right people into our lives by being the right person.

In conclusion, attracting the right people into our lives and businesses is essential for success. It requires clarity, persistence, patience, and a willingness to step outside our comfort zones. By being mindful of whom we attract, and ensuring we are the right person ourselves, we can build a supportive and enriching network that aids in our journey towards success.

Action Steps for Success: Crafting Your Ideal Network

Feeling inspired to surround yourself with the right people? Let's put this into action. Here's a simple yet effective exercise from RAD Strategic Partners to get you started on building your dream network.

Action Item: Identify Your Ideal Connections

1. **Reflect on Your Network:** Think about your current network. Who energizes you? Who drains your energy?
2. **Write Down Your Ideal Traits:** List the qualities of the ideal people you want to surround yourself with. What types of individuals would help you grow, challenge you, and support your dreams? Be as detailed as possible.
3. **Evaluate and Adjust:** Compare your current network with the list of ideal traits you've written. Identify gaps and think about ways you can start attracting these ideal connections into your life.
4. **Create an Action Plan:** Set a goal for the next month to actively seek out and engage with people who embody these traits. This could be through networking events, social media connections, or community gatherings.

Why this Works As we emphasize at RAD Strategic Partners, proactively shaping your network is a crucial step toward RADical success. By intentionally seeking out and connecting with individuals who align with your values and aspirations, you're not just expanding your network—you're strategically positioning yourself for growth and success. Remember, the company you keep can have a profound impact on your journey, so choose wisely and take deliberate steps to cultivate a network that reflects your ambitions and values.

Week 29

FIND YOUR TRIBE:
FOSTERING POWERFUL CONNECTIONS
FOR RADICAL SUCCESS

It Takes a Village

The most successful people in the world, the ones winning the game of life and living lives full of joy and accomplishment, didn't get there independently. They built a tribe of people who supported and helped them achieve their goals and dreams.

The Essence of a Tribe

Building the tribe we need is crucial to personal and professional development. A tribe is a group of people with similar values, goals, and aspirations. It is a support system that provides feedback, encouragement, and growth opportunities. We form our tribe in many ways, such as through family, friends, colleagues, or mastermind groups.[17]

Reflect on Your Tribe

Have we given any thought to our tribe lately? Do we have the tribe we need, and are we accepting their support and nurturing them

---

[17] https://www.naphill.org/focus-instructors/mastermind/

in return? It is worth periodically considering our network, village, team, and tribe and taking a moment to build the tribe we need.

Building and Nurturing Your Tribe

1. **Identify Your Tribe's Characteristics**
   - Determine what type of tribe you need for personal, business, or family growth.
   - Define the values, skills, and personalities that constitute your ideal tribe.
2. **Find Like-Minded People**
   - Attend events, join online communities, and engage with industry peers.
   - Connect and nurture relationships with those who align with your values and goals.
3. **Set Clear Expectations and Protocols**
   - Establish guidelines for communication, behavior, and accountability.
   - Define roles, responsibilities, and decision-making processes.
4. **Involve Everyone in Action Planning**
   - Align your tribe with your vision and goals.
   - Ensure all members understand their roles and responsibilities.
5. **Lead and Support Your Tribe**
   - Set the tone for open communication and accountability.
   - Celebrate successes and recognize individual contributions.

Whether your tribe is a team to grow your business, a family to boost your heart, or a mastermind group to develop yourself, the questions and traits are the same. Surround yourself with people who share your core values, care about your well-being, provide honest feedback, help when needed, show you opportunities, and alert you to risks.

Building the tribe we need is essential to personal and professional growth. It takes effort, commitment, and dedication to identify the type of tribe we need, seek out the right people, establish clear expectations, involve everyone in setting clear action plans, and lead and nurture our tribe. When we have the right tribe, it provides the support and encouragement we need to achieve our goals, live a fulfilling life, build a fantastic business, and achieve RADical success.

Find Your Tribe

Action Steps for Tribe Building

Create Your Tribe Blueprint

1. **List Your Ideal Tribe Members**: Note the traits and characteristics of individuals you want in your tribe. Think about the skills, values, and personalities that would complement and enhance your goals.
2. **Evaluate Your Current Circle**: Compare your current network with your ideal tribe list. Identify who already fits and where there are gaps.
3. **Develop a Plan**: Create a strategy for connecting with potential tribe members. This could include attending specific events, participating in online forums, or reaching out to individuals who embody your desired qualities.

Why It Matters As we at RAD Strategic Partners always say, building your tribe is fundamental to RADical success. By intentionally seeking individuals who align with your goals and values, you're laying the foundation for a support system to empower and elevate your journey. Remember, the strength of your tribe reflects the strength of your success. So, take deliberate steps to cultivate your tribe, and watch how it transforms your path toward achievement.

Week 30

REWARD YOUR TEAM: WHY IT MATTERS AND HOW TO DO IT RIGHT

The Importance of Employee Appreciation

Rewarding your team is a crucial component of a successful business. Not only does it create a positive work environment, but it also motivates and inspires your team to continue to perform at their best. Unfortunately, an annual survey of employees in the US routinely shows a majority of them do not feel appreciated. The survey highlights the need for leaders to change this dynamic and prioritize rewarding their team year-round.[18]

The Impact of Rewarding Your Team

Multiple studies show the importance of rewarding your team. Here are a few examples showing its importance:

1. **Employee Preferences**: A Glassdoor study found that 80% of employees prefer perks over a pay raise.[19]

---

[18] https://www.achievers.com/resources/white-papers/workforce-institute-2023-engagement-and-retention/
[19] https://www.glassdoor.com/blog/ecs-q3-2015/

2. **Engagement and Productivity**: Bersin & Associates noted a 14% increase in these areas in companies that recognize employees regularly.[20]

3. **Financial Results**: Globoforce's research showed that companies investing 1% or more of payroll in recognition are 79% more likely to see better financial outcomes.[21]

4. **Motivation and Loyalty**: Harvard Business Review reported that recognized employees are more motivated and likely to stay longer with the company.[22]

Rewarding your team creates a positive work environment and increases employee engagement and productivity, leading to better business outcomes.

Who Is Your Team?

When we talk about a team, we mean everyone around you who helps you succeed and reach your goals. The list might include employees, coworkers, family members, strategic alliances, referral partners, business partners, and anyone who supports you when needed. There are many ways to reward your team.

Five Effective Ways to Reward Your Team

1. **Pay Appropriately**: Include bonuses, raises, and competitive fees.

2. **Express Gratitude**: A simple "thank you" can significantly impact team morale.

3. **Utilize CNEs (Critical Nonessentials):** Small gestures like lunch treats or unique parking spots can make a big difference.

---

[20] https://www.prnewswire.com/news-releases/bersin--associates-unlocks-the-secrets-of-effective-employee-recognition-158548395.html

[21] https://press.workhuman.com/press-releases/globoforce-recognition-employees/

[22] https://hbr.org/2022/10/a-better-way-to-recognize-your-employees

4. **Acknowledge Accomplishments**: Use awards and public recognition to celebrate hard work.
5. **Offer Services**: Acts of kindness like offering a ride can show deep appreciation.

Personalized Rewards Matter

To be successful, rewards need to be genuine and meaningful to the person receiving them, and they should come from our hearts and not a sense of obligation. A reward needs to be personal and customized to the person receiving it. Understanding your team and what motivates them is crucial to finding a suitable reward.

The Ripple Effect of Rewarding Your Team

Rewarding your team can have numerous benefits for individuals and the organization. When employees feel appreciated and recognized for their hard work and contributions, they tend to have higher levels of job satisfaction and engagement, leading to increased productivity, better customer service, and a stronger loyalty to the company. Rewards can also help to foster a positive work culture and improve teamwork and collaboration among colleagues. Additionally, recognizing and rewarding employees can help attract and retain top talent, as people like to work at companies that value and appreciate their employees.

A Year-Round Commitment

In summary, rewarding your team throughout the year can make all the difference in creating a positive and productive work environment. It shows appreciation for your team's hard work and dedication and can also increase employee morale, reduce turnover, and ultimately contribute to the company's success. By prioritizing the well-being and satisfaction of your team, you are investing in the future of your business. So, take the time to show your team they are valued, and watch the positive effects ripple through the workplace.

Action Steps for Rewarding Your Team

Reflect and Act on Team Rewards

1. **Identify Individual Motivators**: Assess what unique rewards and recognition resonate with each team member. Understand their preferences and aspirations.
2. **Plan Personalized Rewards**: Develop a strategy for personalized appreciation. This could range from handwritten notes to specific rewards aligning with their interests or achievements.
3. **Implement and Evaluate**: Put your reward plan into action and observe the impact. Seek feedback from your team on the effectiveness of the rewards.

Why This Matters At RAD Strategic Partners, we believe understanding your team's unique needs and preferences is crucial for effective reward. By tailoring your appreciation strategies, you make each team member feel valued and foster a culture of recognition and motivation. Remember, when your team feels genuinely appreciated, their productivity, loyalty, and overall satisfaction soar, paving the way for RADical success in your business. So, take the time to thoughtfully reward your team and observe the positive changes in your work environment.

Month 8

COMMUNICATION IS KEY

Mastering the Art of Communication: The RADical Success Dialogue

Welcome to the world of words, where communication reigns supreme. This section is an expedition into the heart of how we connect, influence, and understand each other. It's not just about talking; it's about genuinely communicating in an effective, empathetic, and empowering way.

We begin by breaking the ice—the art of starting conversations that matter. You'll learn techniques for opening engaging and meaningful dialogues with new clients, potential partners, and team members.

Next, we dive into the nuances of making conversation. This isn't just chitchat; it's about crafting memorable and impactful conversations and forging lasting connections.

In our digital age, the rules of communication have evolved. We'll explore the do's and don'ts of digital dialogue—how to be clear, concise, and courteous in a world where your words are often typed, not spoken.

Then comes the cornerstone of all excellent communication—listening. Authentic listening is an active, participatory process. You'll learn how to listen not just with your ears but with your heart and mind.

Lastly, we explore the power of asking—the simple act of seeking to understand before seeking to be understood. Questions are the bridge to deeper insights and connections.

Ready to amplify your communication skills? This section will transform you from just another speaker to a master communicator in your journey to RADical Success. Let's talk the talk and walk the walk, shall we?

COMMUNICATION
IS
THE
RESPONSE
YOU
GET

Week 31

BREAK THE ICE: MASTERING THE ART OF NETWORKING FOR RADICAL SUCCESS

Networking is vital in achieving RADical success, whether it's expanding your business, finding new opportunities, or creating meaningful connections. Remember, it's not just about the size of your village but the strength of your bonds within it. In this digital age, while many opportunities are just a click away, the art of face-to-face networking remains invaluable.

The Essence of Networking

Networking isn't just about accumulating contacts; it's about cultivating relationships. It involves consistent engagement, a willingness to step out of your comfort zone, and the ability to initiate conversations. The best networkers don't wait for opportunities but create them.

Ice-Breaker Questions: Your Networking Toolkit

To make your networking efforts more effective, having a set of engaging questions is essential. These questions can open up conversations, allowing you to learn about others and explore potential collaboration opportunities.

- **Career Path:** What inspired you to choose your current career path?
- **Expertise:** What unique skills make you excel in what you do?
- **Ambitions:** If guaranteed success, what's one thing you'd love to try?
- **Personal Experiences:** Can you share an unexpected or amusing incident from your life?
- **Current Challenges:** What's the biggest hurdle you're facing right now?
- **Guidance:** What advice would you give to newcomers in your field?
- **Passion for Profession:** What aspect of your work brings you the most joy?

Active Listening: The Key to Effective Networking

The magic of networking lies in listening. By showing genuine interest in others, you gather insights and establish yourself as someone who values connections over transactions. Remember, effective networking is as much about being interested as being interesting.

Networking in Action

Networking is an ongoing process. Follow these steps to maximize your networking efforts:

1. **Consistency:** Regularly attend events and engage with new people.
2. **Initiation:** Don't hesitate to approach others. Use your ice-breaker questions to start discussions.
3. **Two-Way Engagement:** Ensure your conversations are balanced. Share about yourself, but more importantly, show interest in others.

4. **Follow Up:** Post-event, reach out to those you met. A simple message referencing your conversation can be a great start to a lasting relationship.
5. **Preparation:** Always have a few conversation starters ready. This shows you're prepared and genuinely interested in engaging.

Cultivating Your Network Garden

Building a strong network is like tending a garden. It requires nurturing, patience, and regular attention. You plant seeds of potential collaborations, partnerships, and friendships by actively engaging in conversations, listening attentively, and following up. Over time, these seeds can grow into a thriving network that supports your personal and professional growth.

Remember, every individual you meet has a unique story and perspective. By embracing the art of networking and breaking the ice effectively, you open doors to a world of opportunities and inch closer to achieving your RADical success.

Action Steps: Elevating Your Networking Game

Ready to transform your networking approach and achieve RADical success? It's time for action. Follow these steps to hone your networking skills and build a robust, supportive network.

1. **Reflect on Your Current Network:** Make a list of your existing network connections. Are there gaps in your network that need filling?
2. **Set Networking Goals:** Define clear, achievable objectives for your networking activities. Are you looking to expand your business, find a mentor, or explore new career opportunities?
3. **Plan Your Networking Activities:** Identify upcoming networking events, online forums, or social gatherings relevant to your goals. Mark them in your calendar.
4. **Develop Conversation Starters:** Based on your networking goals, prepare a list of tailored ice-breaker questions. Practice them.
5. **Engage, Listen, and Follow Up:** At your next networking event, use your conversation starters. After the event, follow up with new connections within forty-eight hours.

Why This Matters At RAD Strategic Partners, we understand the power of a strong network. It's not just about collecting contacts; it's about creating meaningful relationships that support and enrich your journey towards success. By taking these actionable steps, you're not just expanding your network but strategically building a community that resonates with your personal and professional aspirations. Implement these steps consistently and watch your network transform into a valuable asset in pursuing RADical success.

Week 32

CONVERSE FOR SUCCESS: EXCELLING AT CONVERSATIONAL SKILLS IN BUSINESS

Conversational skills are more critical than ever in our increasingly complex and interconnected business world. They are vital to creating a positive work environment, building relationships, resolving conflicts, and creating new business opportunities. Engaging effectively with colleagues, clients, and prospects is a professional must-have skill.

Establishing Rapport and Building Trust

Conversational skills enable us to establish rapport and create a relaxed atmosphere for openly sharing thoughts and ideas. They are instrumental in building trust—a fundamental component of any successful relationship. By enhancing our conversational skills, we can accelerate trust-building and relationship formation.

Understanding Needs and Creating Opportunities

Practical conversational skills help us better understand our clients' and prospects' needs and wants. We can develop better solutions and create new business opportunities by asking insightful questions and actively listening.

Tips to Improve Conversational Skills and Communication

1. **Listen Actively:** Focus on the other person's words and respond thoughtfully. Avoid interrupting or finishing their sentences.
2. **Ask Open-Ended Questions:** Encourage open sharing by asking questions that require more than a "yes" or "no" answer.
3. **Practice Empathy:** Understand and show empathy towards the other person's perspective.
4. **Avoid Jargon:** Use simple language to be easily understood by everyone.
5. **Mind Your Body Language:** Be aware of nonverbal cues and ensure they match your intended message.
6. **Practice Regularly:** Strengthen your conversational skills through regular practice in various settings.

Staying Informed and Conversational in Current Affairs

Being well-informed about current events and industry news is crucial. It enhances your professional knowledge and provides material for engaging conversations.

Mastering Conversational Skills on Zoom

In the virtual work environment, effective communication over video calls is essential. Here are some tips for excelling in virtual conversations:

- Test audio and video settings before the call.
- Dress appropriately and maintain a professional demeanor.
- Focus on maintaining eye contact by looking into the camera.
- Be conscious of body language, even in a virtual setting.
- Use nonverbal cues for interaction, and avoid interrupting.

The Impact of Strong Conversational Skills

By honing our conversational skills, we can become more effective communicators, which in turn helps us build stronger relationships with colleagues, clients, and potential business partners. Effective conversation is a cornerstone of success in any business setting, from networking events to one-on-one meetings and even in the virtual realm of video calls. These skills help make a positive impression and are instrumental in achieving business goals and fostering successful professional relationships.

Learn to Converse

Action Steps: Elevating Your Conversational Skills

You're equipped with the knowledge, but how do you turn it into action? Let's dive into practical steps to elevate your conversational skills:

Daily Exercise for Conversational Muscle

1. **Active Listening Drills:** Practice active listening in everyday conversations. Focus on understanding, not just hearing.
2. **Question Quest:** Daily, ask one open-ended question in your conversations and observe the responses. Note what works and what doesn't.
3. **Empathy Challenge:** Each day, try to understand and verbalize the perspective of at least one person you converse with.
4. **Jargon Jar:** Every time you catch yourself using jargon, put a coin in a jar. It's a fun way to become more aware of your language.
5. **Body Language Awareness:** In every conversation, be conscious of your body language. Practice open, engaging gestures.
6. **Zoom Mastery:** Schedule a mock Zoom call weekly to practice your virtual communication skills. Record and review.

Tracking Progress: Keep a conversation journal. Note your daily conversational interactions, what you learned, and how to improve.

Remember, as we say at RAD Strategic Partners, mastering the art of conversation is a journey, not a destination. By continuously honing your skills, you're setting the stage for RADical success in all aspects of your professional life. Every conversation is an opportunity to grow—seize it!

Week 33

COMMUNICATION BREAKDOWN: A SURVIVAL GUIDE FOR THE DIGITAL ERA

In today's fast-paced world, we constantly need to communicate in new and innovative ways. In a post-pandemic environment, millions of people have had to adapt to remote work and figure out how to collaborate effectively from separate locations. But you know what? This isn't the first time we've had to navigate such challenges.

The Evolution of Communication Tools

Believe it or not, throughout the past fifty years, there have been numerous technological advancements that have revolutionized the way we communicate—from computers and fax machines to email, conference lines, PDAs, video calling, and now, masks. It's safe to say that the communication landscape has undergone RADical transformations in the past few decades.

The Challenge of Digital Communication

While these technological marvels have provided us with fantastic tools for virtual communication and remote work, none of them can truly replicate the experience of face-to-face interaction. After all, when we engage in a conversation with someone, it's not just the words we use that convey meaning. Our tone and body language play a significant role in effective communication. Unfortunately, in written communication like emails, we're limited to expressing ourselves through words alone. This calls for choosing our words wisely and considering how different recipients may interpret them. On the other hand, verbal communication, such as phone calls or conference calls, allows for both tone and words, but we mustn't forget that half of our communication is conveyed through body language. Body language encompasses facial expressions and posture, so video conferencing tools like Zoom have become invaluable in overcoming some of these challenges.

Adapting to Different Communication Styles

However, effective communication isn't solely dependent on the tools we use; it also relies on the recipient. We all process information differently, and it's crucial to bear that in mind when giving instructions or conveying messages. The way we communicate reflects in the response we receive, and it's essential to recognize that when others are trying to fulfill our requests, they aim to please us. Therefore, if the outcome doesn't meet our expectations, we should consider that the breakdown might lie in the communication itself. It's incredible how three people can interpret the same instruction in three entirely different ways. I won't even get started on my husband attempting to follow a baking recipe!

Strategies for Effective Digital Communication

When the results of our communication fall short, it's time to reassess and adapt our approach. In the absence of face-to-face contact, it becomes crucial to check in more frequently. Don't be afraid to reach out and ask for or provide updates. Confirm priorities, deadlines, and expectations with your fellow team members. Embrace technology in all its diverse forms to stay connected with people and foster effective communication. And never underestimate the power of seeking feedback. If the instructions you give don't yield the desired results, it's time to rewrite them! Don't let a communication breakdown happen to you.

Overcoming Communication Barriers

1. If the person you are trying to contact doesn't respond at first, try reaching out via a different channel. Sometimes, a quick phone call or a well-crafted email can make all the difference.
2. Avoid repeating the same instruction verbatim if the outcome isn't what you desired. Instead, rephrase it. Try approaching the topic differently or providing more context to ensure clarity.
3. Consider using a tool like DISC to better understand different communication styles and how to adapt to them. Want to learn more about your own style? Take a DISC assessment and receive a comprehensive report, including your style and how to communicate with others.

Remember, effective communication is a continuous learning, adapting, and refining process. By embracing new technologies, understanding different communication styles, and remaining open to feedback, you'll be well on your way to overcoming any communication hurdles that come your way.

So, go forth and conquer the world of communication. Break down those barriers, bridge those gaps, and make connections that transcend distance and circumstances. Communication breakdown? Not on your watch!

Take a DISC Assessment

Action Plan to Boost Digital Communication

1. **Reflect and Identify Weaknesses:** Take a moment to reflect on your recent digital communications. Identify instances where the message might not have been clear or was misunderstood.

2. **Experiment with Different Communication Channels:** Over the next week, use various communication methods like emails, phone calls, or video conferences for different messages—notice which method yields the best response and clarity.

3. **Active Listening and Feedback Gathering:** Focus on active listening during your next few conversations. After the conversation, ask for feedback on your communication's clarity and effectiveness.

4. **Implement DISC Assessment:** Visit our site to take a DISC assessment. Understand your communication style and learn how to adapt to others' styles.

5. **Adapt Your Approach:** Adapt your communication approach based on feedback and your DISC assessment results. If a method doesn't work, try rephrasing or choosing a different communication channel.

Why This Matters: As we embrace the principles outlined in RAD Strategic Partners, it becomes evident that mastering digital communication is not a one-time task but an ongoing journey. Each step we take towards understanding and improving our communication styles brings us closer to RADical success in our professional and personal lives.

Week 34

LISTEN MORE: UNLOCKING DEEPER CONNECTIONS THROUGH ACTIVE LISTENING

One of the secrets to RADical success in sales, leadership, business, and life is the quality of the relationships you build with others. Relationships matter both to your success and to the quality of your life. The relationships with your family, team, peers, vendors, friends, and customers directly impact your success. How do you build these relationships? What if you only have a few minutes to make an impression deep enough to encourage engagement?

The Art of Active Listening

Listening to people when they speak goes a long way in forging a bond. We all think we listen when we have conversations, but do we? Are we fully present, giving our full attention to the other person, or are we distracted by our environment or the meeting to which we are running late? Are we focused on ourselves and our responses? When we become effective listeners, our relationships deepen, and our results skyrocket.

Build Strong Relationships Through Listening

- **Focus Attention:** Truly listening means being present in the conversation, not preoccupied with your next meeting or response. This focused attention is fundamental to deepening relationships.
- **Encourage Conversation:** Instead of saying, "I know," use phrases like "tell me more" to keep the conversation flowing and demonstrate genuine interest.
- **Engage Intelligently:** Ask thoughtful questions to show you're engaged and interested in understanding their perspective.
- **Minimize Distractions:** Whether in person or on a video call, maintain eye contact and avoid checking your watch or phone. Your undivided attention speaks volumes.
- **Build Conversational Flow:** Replace dismissive terms like but or however with and or in addition to build upon the conversation instead of contradicting it.

Active listening is a learned art that would be well worth your time to practice. The more we listen, the more we learn, connect, and grow. It may seem like an effort, but it pays off in so many ways. Here is an easy example of the benefits of active listening that you can try immediately:

One of my current talents is my ability to remember people's names. People ask me all the time to share my secret for remembering names. When I first got into coaching, I knew that I was not very good at remembering names and thought this was something I should develop. I looked for the answer and concluded I wasn't paying attention when people introduced themselves. I decided to pay attention when people were introduced or introduced themselves. From that day forward, I became very good at remembering names. Try this yourself. The next time you are out, decide to pay attention and then watch how many new names you recall.

Engage and connect by listening more than you speak. Be open to what people are saying, and don't block them out just because you disagree with what they are saying. You might learn something. Ask questions and let people know you are listening to them. Ask them to clarify points about which you are not clear. Restate facts you want to confirm. These are all keys to clear communication. You may be surprised by what you hear when you listen.

Listening is one of the greatest secrets to successful leadership, sales, careers, and relationships. The best listeners have the best results. When you pay attention to others, you connect, engage, build connections, and solve problems for others and yourself.

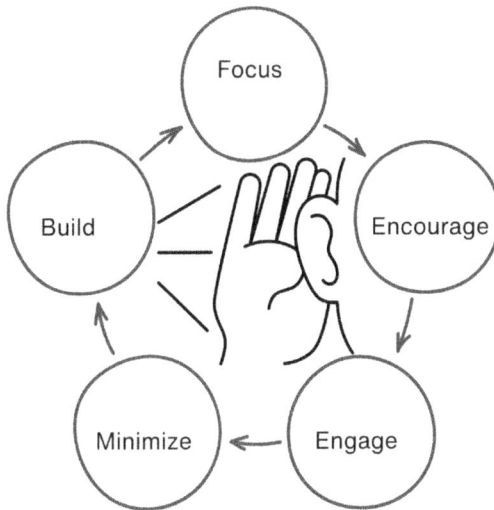

Action Section: Enhance Your Listening Skills

1. **Name Recall:**
   - Make a conscious effort to remember names in your next social or business gathering. Pay attention when introductions are made, and use names during the conversation.
2. **Active Engagement Exercise:**
   - In your next conversation, focus solely on listening. Avoid planning your response while the other person is speaking. After the conversation, jot down key points you remember.
3. **Feedback Gathering:**
   - After a significant conversation, ask for feedback on how effectively you listened. Were you attentive, did you understand their points, and did they feel heard?

Why This Matters: At RAD Strategic Partners, we understand that active listening is a skill that enhances every aspect of your professional and personal life. By improving your listening skills, you build stronger relationships and gain deeper insights and understanding, leading to more informed decisions and actions.

Week 35

MASTER THE POWER OF ASKING: UNLOCKING SUCCESS, TEA, AND MAGIC

A fundamental habit of success is regularly and routinely asking for what you want. It sounds so simple, doesn't it? Just ask, and you might get it. But let's face it, asking for what we want is easier said than done. We pride ourselves on our independence and self-reliance. We're strong and powerful and believe we don't need any help! After all, that's why we own businesses and have amazingly successful careers, right?

Embracing the Courage to Ask

Well, here's a little secret: while we might be capable of achieving our goals without help, doing so actually holds us back. Sure, we may not need assistance, but we can certainly get there faster and more easily with some support. So, let me ask: do you ask for what you want or settle for the status quo?

A Cup of Tea and the Art of Asking

Picture this: one weekend, I found myself at a conference. The organizer had put out coffee, but as luck would have it, I'm not a coffee person. I prefer a good ol' cup of tea. So, on the first day, I couldn't help but feel a twinge of disappointment all day long—no tea for me to enjoy. However, when I saw someone come to refresh the coffee station on the second day, I mustered up the courage to ask for help. "Is it possible to get tea instead of coffee?" I inquired, holding my breath. To my surprise, the person responded, "Sure, what type of tea would you like? I'll bring a few tea bags and a carafe of hot water." Just like that, it happened. I wanted something, I asked for it, and the tea magically appeared.

From Tea to Book Forewords

The real magic happens when you ask for what you want. Let me share another story with you. When I wrote my first book, I decided to aim high. I asked Jack Canfield, coauthor of Chicken Soup for the Soul, to write a foreword for my book. You might expect such a successful author to decline such a request, but guess what? He was more than happy to contribute. Throughout my life, I've learned that help was often granted when I summoned the courage to ask for it. You see, you get more of what you want, and you get it faster when you master this simple habit.

Overcoming the Mindset of Lack

So, why do we often hold ourselves back from asking? The answer lies in a place of lack—a mindset that limits us. We're afraid to ask for a whole bunch of reasons we make up in our heads. Maybe they're too busy. Perhaps the ask is too big, and they cannot afford to help us. Perhaps we believe we don't deserve it. But here's the truth: these are all statements of lack and scarcity. They stem from a place of believing there isn't enough, and perhaps we can't have everything we want.

The Abundance of the World: A Shift in Focus

But let me tell you something, the world works in abundance, not lack. Wherever you focus your attention and energy, the results are amplified. If you search for reasons why people can't give you what you want, you'll find them and create more of those reasons.

However, if you shift your focus to asking for what you want, you'll find that you get more of what you want more often than not.

Putting the Habit into Practice

Start asking for what you want from people who might be able to give it to you. If the options presented aren't quite what you're looking for, ask if alternatives are possible. Whether in your business or personal life, ask anyone you can how they might help, and you'll discover the answers you need to achieve all your goals. We live in a connected society where knowledge and skill sharing are becoming more and more common. Believe it or not, people want to help you find success. Show them how they can.

Now, let me leave you with a few questions to ponder: What are you missing out on by not asking for what you want in your business? What risks do you take by not asking for help? Think about the valuable time you spend doing and learning things yourself when you could simply ask for assistance. And finally, what is the first thing you will ask for after reading this message?

Remember, the art of asking is a pathway to success and a gateway to tea, magic, and all the extraordinary things you desire. Embrace it and watch how your world transforms.

Your Next Step: Unleash the Magic of Asking

Unlock the potential in every opportunity by mastering the art of asking. This simple yet powerful habit can lead you to success, new possibilities, and even a magical cup of tea. Embrace it fully and watch as your world transforms with each request you make.

- **Exercise:** Think of a situation where you hesitated to ask for help. Write down what you wanted to ask and identify whom you could have asked.
- **Next Step:** Approach someone this week with a request or question to help you move forward in your business or personal life. Notice how this act changes the outcome.
- **Reflection:** After you've made your request, reflect on how it felt and the response you received. Did it lead to a positive outcome or learning experience?

Why are we doing this? Asking for help or what you need is a strength, not a weakness. It opens doors to growth, learning, and success. Keep this habit at the forefront of your interactions and see how it transforms your journey to success.

Month 9

UNDERSTAND SALES

Sales as a Life Skill: Navigating the Marketplace of RADical Success

Welcome to the dynamic world of sales, where the ability to influence, persuade, and connect is the key to unlocking life and business achievements. This section isn't just about selling products or services; it's about understanding sales as a fundamental skill for success in all arenas.

First up, we demystify marketing. It's essential, not just as a business tool, but as a means of communicating your value to the world. Effective marketing is the starting block of any successful venture, whether you're promoting a product, idea, or personal brand.

Embracing your uniqueness is where the magic happens. Your unique value proposition sets you apart in a world saturated with choices. You'll learn to harness your individuality as your greatest sales asset.

Next, we explore strategies to open doors, make connections, and create opportunities where others see none. It's about not waiting for chances but building them.

Finally, we delve into the art of selling your way to success. Sales is not just an exchange of goods; it's an exchange of ideas, value, and solutions. It's about solving problems and creating satisfying experiences.

Whether you're a seasoned sales professional or you've never thought of yourself as a salesperson, this section will equip you with the tools and insights to sell your way to RADical success. Ready to turn every "no" into a potential "yes"? Let's dive in.

> "
> *Everyone lives by selling something.*
> "

-Robert Louis Stevenson

Week 36

MARKETING IS ESSENTIAL: UNLOCK STRATEGIES TO BOOST YOUR BOTTOM LINE

Marketing is the backbone of any successful business. It's the process of promoting and selling products or services through various channels to attract customers and create brand awareness. Due to limited resources, time, and budget, marketing can be daunting for small businesses. However, it's essential to remember that marketing is not an expense; it's an investment that can lead to significant growth and profitability. Here are some ways to successfully market your business or yourself.

Importance of Marketing for Small Businesses Marketing is crucial for our businesses for several reasons. First, it helps us create brand awareness and differentiate ourselves. With so many options available to consumers, we must stand out and showcase our unique value proposition. Second, marketing allows businesses to connect with their target audience and build relationships with potential customers. It's not just about selling a product or service; it's about creating an emotional connection with our customers to keep them coming back. Third, marketing can lead to increased sales and revenue. Small businesses can grow their customer base and increase profits by attracting and retaining new customers.

Eye-Opening Statistics on Marketing for Small Businesses

- Only 50% of small businesses survive their first five years. One of the main reasons for failure is a lack of marketing.[23]
- 61% of small businesses don't have a formalized marketing plan.[24]
- 81% of consumers research a product or service online before purchasing.[25]
- 73% of consumers say they would rather learn about a product or service through video.[26]
- Email marketing has an ROI of 4,400%.[27]

Actionable Steps for You to Improve Your Marketing

1. **Develop a Marketing Plan:** As mentioned above, 61% of small businesses don't have a formalized marketing plan. A marketing plan is a roadmap that outlines your marketing strategy, target audience, budget, and goals. Without a plan, it's easy to get sidetracked and waste resources on ineffective marketing tactics.
2. **Define Your Target Audience:** Knowing your target audience is crucial to creating effective marketing campaigns. Understanding their needs, wants, and pain points is essential to crafting messaging that resonates with

---

[23] https://www.bls.gov/bdm/entrepreneurship/entrepreneurship.htm
[24] https://servicedirect.com/resources/small-business-content-marketing-survey-data/
[25] https://chainstoreage.com/news/study-81-research-online-making-big-purchases/
[26] https://blog.hubspot.com/marketing/hubspot-blog-social-media-marketing-report
[27] https://www.statista.com/statistics/804656/email-roi-perception/#:~:text=During%20a%202020%20survey%20carried,dollars%20per%20one%20dollar%20spent

them. Utilize tools like social media analytics and customer surveys to gather insights into your target audience.

3. **Utilize Social Media:** Social media is a powerful tool small businesses can use to reach their target audience. With billions of social media users worldwide, it's essential to have a solid social media presence. Create a social media strategy that includes the platforms your target audience uses and the content that resonates with them.

4. **Create Engaging Content:** Content marketing is crucial to any marketing strategy. Creating engaging content that educates, informs, and entertains your target audience can help build brand awareness and trust. Utilize different types of content, such as blog posts, videos, infographics, and podcasts, to reach your audience.

5. **Optimize Your Website:** A website is often the first interaction a potential customer has with your business. It's essential to optimize your website for search engines and be user-friendly and mobile-responsive. Utilize tools like Google Analytics to track website traffic and user behavior to improve your website's performance.

6. **Leverage Email Marketing:** Email marketing is a cost-effective way to reach and engage your target audience. Create targeted email campaigns that deliver personalized content and promotions to your subscribers. Utilize tools like Mailchimp or Constant Contact to manage your email marketing campaigns.

7. **Utilize Paid Advertising:** While organic marketing tactics are essential, paid advertising can quickly help businesses reach a broader audience. Utilize platforms like Google Ads, Facebook Ads, Instagram Ads, and other new platforms as they develop.

In conclusion, marketing is essential for the growth and success of small businesses. With the increasing competition and evolving market, staying ahead and reaching the target audience effectively is crucial. Small businesses can achieve this by understanding their target audience, building a solid brand, and utilizing various marketing channels. Small businesses can attract new customers, retain existing ones, and increase their revenue by developing and consistently implementing a solid marketing plan.

Although marketing may seem overwhelming, it is essential to remember that it is an ongoing process. Small businesses can stay relevant and successful by continuously analyzing the results and adapting the strategies accordingly. So, take the time to evaluate your marketing efforts and adjust them as necessary. With dedication, persistence, and the right approach, any small business can achieve marketing success and grow to new heights.

Marketing is essential for reaching our audience, but to truly stand out, we must highlight our distinctive edge. It's not enough to market our products and services; we must also emphasize what makes us unique in the crowded marketplace.

Action Section: Empower Your Marketing Strategy

You're now equipped to understand why marketing is vital to your business's success. But knowledge without action is like a book that's never read. So, what's the next step? Let's dive in and apply these insights to fuel your growth.

Action Item: Craft Your Marketing Blueprint

1. **Reflect and Identify:** Take a moment to reflect on your current marketing efforts. What strategies have you tried? What worked and what didn't? Identify unexplored opportunities or areas needing improvement.
2. **Draft a Basic Marketing Plan:** Create a simple marketing plan if you don't have one. Outline your goals, target audience, budget, and key strategies. This plan will be your roadmap, guiding you toward more structured and focused marketing efforts.
3. **Engage with Your Audience:** Connect with your audience through social media or direct interactions. Gather feedback, understand their needs, and tailor your approach accordingly.
4. **Experiment and Learn:** Choose one new marketing channel or strategy to try this month. It could be a new social media platform, an email campaign, or even paid advertising. The goal is to expand your reach and learn from new experiences.

Why We Do This: As we always say at RAD Strategic Partners, proactive marketing is your business's growth lifeline. By deliberately enhancing your marketing, you're not just casting a wider net but building a stronger foundation for sustained success.

Week 37

UNLEASH YOUR DISTINCTIVE EDGE: HARNESS YOUR UNIQUE TALENTS

The Dilemma of Distinctiveness

As we navigate the world's complexities, the tension between blending in and standing out becomes palpable. Within this dichotomy lies a profound question: what makes you unique? Amidst the societal pressures to conform lies the potential for RADical success, all tied to embracing our individuality.

In a sea of uniformity, our distinct qualities become our superpower. Consider the business landscape: companies that resonate most with consumers aren't just those offering products or services but those exuding an unmistakable brand identity. They are the companies that promise overnight shipping to deliver delight or craft devices emphasizing simplicity and beauty.

This ethos translates seamlessly into the professional sphere. Climbing the corporate ladder is not solely about ticking the performance checkboxes. The individuals who infuse their roles with distinctive talents and perspectives rise to the top. To land that dream job or secure that promotion, leading with what sets you apart while still adhering to the necessary rules of the game, is crucial.

Mastering the Balancing Act

Understanding where to draw the line is a skill that the most successful individuals have mastered. They know how to navigate the tight and loose rules within their environments—adhering to the nonnegotiables while artfully bending the malleable to illuminate their individuality.

Strategies for Illuminating Your Individuality

1. **Decipher the Rules:** Grasp the nonnegotiable "tight rules" and the malleable "loose rules" of your target environment. For instance, while a corporate dress code can be interpreted with some creative liberties, stepping out of bounds in sports or failing to pay your mortgage has unequivocal consequences.
2. **Leverage Your Strengths:** Invest time in understanding your inherent strengths and passions. Leading with your innate talents and continuously honing them allows you to navigate your career and life with your unique flair.
3. **Employ Your Distinct Assets:** Embrace and proudly utilize whatever makes you stand out. Whether it's intellect, charisma, resilience, or creativity, let these attributes be the pillars of your personal and professional life.
4. **Dare to Be Noticeable:** The definitions of success vary, but at its core, it's about fully utilizing your abilities to lead a life rich in purpose, happiness, and influence. We naturally distinguish ourselves from the crowd when we adopt this view of success.

Suppose your aspiration is a fulfilling business, a progressive career, or a life lived to the fullest. You'll need courage to step into the spotlight and move beyond average. By ardently pursuing your ambitions and employing your unique gifts, you can carve out a journey that is unmistakably your own. Here, on this authentic path, you make your indelible mark.

In conclusion, the secret sauce to RADical success is no enigma. It's a bold embrace of what makes you distinct, coupled with the wisdom to know how to maneuver within the frameworks of society. It's about standing out with intention and letting your unique light shine in a way that brings about your definition of success. After all, in a world of replicas, the originals leave a lasting legacy.

Embrace your unique qualities, for they are the keystones to building a life and career that not only stand out but stand the test of time.

Transform Uniqueness into Action

You've read about the power of embracing your uniqueness, but what's the tangible next step to leveraging this for RADical success? Here's a straightforward action item to start with:

Action Item: Identify and Amplify Your Uniqueness Take a moment to reflect and write down three attributes or talents that make you distinct. Next to each, outline how you can amplify this quality in your professional or personal life over the next month. For instance, if you have a knack for creative thinking, plan a brainstorming session where you can lead your team to innovative solutions.

Why this step? At RAD Strategic Partners, we believe self-awareness is the cornerstone of personal growth and professional development. By recognizing what makes you uniquely equipped to excel, you're not just embracing your identity but aligning it with your aspirations for growth and impact. Identifying your unique traits and actively finding ways to enhance their presence in your life puts you on a path not just to success but to RADical success that is authentically yours.

Week 38

OPEN THE DOOR TO OPPORTUNITY: A GUIDE TO SEIZING SUCCESS

Opportunities for achieving RADical success abound in every corner of life. But are we really open to embracing these opportunities? While it's easy to say "yes," we often unwittingly shut doors on them. Recognizing and seizing these opportunities requires awareness and a willingness to act. So, what's the magic formula? Well, it might be simpler than you think.

How to Open Opportunities

The path to opportunities begins with keen observation and active listening, followed by timely action. It's like being on a treasure hunt. With a treasure map in hand, the treasure is not too far away!

Five Tips to Help You Grab Opportunities

1. **Respect Time When Reaching Out:** When contacting someone, always check if it's a good time to call, and then honor their response. We usually contact people at our convenience, not theirs. By respecting their time, you'll notice a significant shift in how receptive they are. It's like having the correct key for the door.

2. **Follow Up When Promised:** If someone tells you they'll be available between ten and twelve o'clock on Thursday, ensure you reach out to them then. Being punctual is like having your foot in the door; it allows you to step into opportunities.

3. **Offer Trial Periods When Possible:** If someone shows interest in your product or service, find a way to let them try it. Long-term contracts are our goal, but trials can be the stepping stones. Think of it as a "test drive" towards success.

4. **Listen and Make Notes:** Whether it's customers, bosses, employees, or prospects, attentive listening helps you respond effectively. Taking notes isn't just for school; it's a strategy that takes you to the head of the class in business.

5. **Ask Questions and Listen to Answers:** Engaging in meaningful dialogue creates a two-way street of opportunity. Ask how you might help others, and don't hesitate to seek help yourself. It's like a dance—both parties lead and follow in turn.

Seizing Opportunity Is about Being Proactive

Finding opportunities isn't akin to waiting for a lucky draw; it's about actively seeking them out. This week, make it a goal to go out and listen with intent. You might be surprised by what you hear. The doors you open could lead to unimagined pathways.

At RAD Strategic Partners, we believe in unlocking those doors and walking the path of opportunity with you. Remember, dear readers, opportunities are everywhere, and the key to unlocking them is within you. So why wait? It's time to open the door to opportunity and walk towards your RADical success!

Action Section: Unlock Your Path to Opportunity

You're now at the threshold of transforming your approach to opportunities. Knowledge is your guide, but action is your key to unlocking the doors of success. So, how do you step forward into a world brimming with potential?

Action Item: Embrace Opportunity with Intention

1. **Evaluate Your Approach:** Reflect on how you've been responding to potential opportunities. Have you been proactive or passive? Identify the moments you might have overlooked and consider what held you back.
2. **Set an Opportunity Goal:** Choose one specific area where you want to improve in seizing opportunities. It could be better networking, being more punctual in follow-ups, or offering trial periods to potential clients.
3. **Create an Opportunity Checklist:** Create a checklist for yourself based on the tips provided. This includes respecting others' time, following up as promised, offering trial periods, attentive listening, and engaging in meaningful dialogues.
4. **Implement and Observe:** For the next two weeks, consciously apply this checklist in your daily interactions. Observe the changes in the responses you receive and the doors that start to open.

Why We Do This: At RAD Strategic Partners, we understand that opportunities are like seeds; they need the right conditions to sprout. By intentionally changing your approach, you're creating a fertile ground for these seeds to grow. Each step you take is sowing the seeds for future success.

Week 39

SELL YOUR WAY TO SUCCESS: WHY SALES SKILLS ARE ESSENTIAL FOR SMALL BUSINESS OWNERS

I know what you are thinking. What? Has Angie lost her mind? What do sales have to do with success? How does sales ability relate to reaching my goals, making my dreams come true, and living a life of passion and purpose? In short, the answer is "everything."

The Vital Role of Sales Skills

Sales is not just a skill; it's an attitude, a mindset, and a way of life. Sales is about connecting with others, understanding their needs, and finding a way to fulfill those needs. Sales is not about pushing products or services but building relationships and providing value.

I talk to people who struggle with sales all the time. Or, more correctly, they think sales is a tricky thing. A slight attitude shift will make a huge difference. Those of us with sales reluctance tend to view these transactions as negative: someone has a product we don't need and is trying to convince us we must have it. A small change in that view will reflect sales in a new light. Sales shows another human that we have the solution to their problem or can assist them in achieving their goals through our unique skills and talents.

The higher our ability to sell our message, product, expertise, and assistance, the more significant our impact will be on the world.

Everyone Is a Great Salesperson

Everyone is a salesperson. Strong sales skills allow us to gain employment of our choosing and get promotions on our timetable. We also use them to connect with others and form partnerships, friendships, families, and relationships. They allow us to start businesses and convince people to work for us. They provide us with the ability to get our children to eat their vegetables, wash their hands, and go to bed at a reasonable time. Our capacity to sell our message determines the likelihood that people will connect with us and work with us in cooperative ways.

For many business owners sales is the most challenging aspect of running a business. But sales is also the most critical aspect of business success. Without sales, there are no customers; without customers, there is no business.

Tips for Boosting Your Sales Skills

1. **Honesty and Integrity:** Act with visible honesty and unspoken integrity. Be the trust you want to experience.
2. **Excitement in Helping Others:** Find excitement in the possibility of helping others, and look for ways to use your skills and talents to do so. You shouldn't be reluctant to sell yourself; you should be delighted.
3. **Active Listening:** Listen more than you speak on every sales call and in every meeting. When you learn to listen to people, it's easy to identify how or if you might be able to help them.
4. **Problem Solving:** Stop selling your wares and start solving people's problems with your product. I don't want a plate. I want someplace pretty to put my food.

5. **Confidence, Not Arrogance:** Act with self-assurance but not arrogance. Be confident in yourself and your product, but don't go too far.
6. **Social Media:** Use social media to your advantage. Using social media as part of your sales strategy is essential to building recognition and generating leads.
7. **Relationship Building:** Focus on building relationships, not making sales. Building relationships leads to repeat business, referrals, and a positive reputation in your industry.

Developing our sales muscle allows us to employ the help of others in achieving our goals while also providing an outlet to use our skills and talents to build a better world. The best salespeople in the world have the most significant impact.

In conclusion, sales is an essential aspect of business success. Whether you are a small business owner, an entrepreneur, or an employee, developing your sales skills will allow you to reach your goals.

Action Item: Elevate Your Sales Insight

Book Recommendation: Purchase *Influence: The Psychology of Persuasion* by Robert Cialdini. It's a transformative read that offers profound insights into the psychology of sales and persuasion.

Read and Reflect: As you read, take notes on how the principles can apply to your business and personal interactions.

Implement One Principle: Choose one principle from the book that resonates with you. Focus on implementing it in your daily interactions, both in business and personal contexts.

Why We Do This: At RAD Strategic Partners, we understand that sales is more than just a business activity; it's a vital skill that permeates every aspect of our lives. By enhancing your sales skills and understanding the psychology behind them, you're boosting your business potential and enriching your personal connections. This week, dive into a new perspective on sales and watch as doors open to RADical success!

Month 10

LEARN TO ADAPT

Adapting to Win: The Ever-Changing Landscape of RADical Success

In this next stretch of our journey, we confront an inescapable truth: the only constant in life and business is change. This section is dedicated to mastering the art of adaptation—a skill as crucial as any strategy or mindset we've explored.

We kick off with the importance of staying current, of keeping your finger on the pulse of industry trends, technological advancements, and societal shifts. It's not just about being informed; it's about being agile and responsive.

Then, we explore how to create abundance with gratitude. It's easy to focus on what we lack or fear losing. Here, we shift the narrative to appreciate what we have and see potential in what's to come. This mindset is a powerful catalyst for attracting more success and joy.

Embracing change is next. As you tolerate the winds of change and set your sails to them, you'll learn to see change not as a threat but as an opportunity for growth, innovation, and reinvention.

Lastly, we tackle conquering your inner victim. Change can be daunting, and retreating into a mindset of helplessness is tempting. We'll discuss strategies to empower you, transforming challenges into stepping stones toward success.

Ready to become a change maestro in the symphony of life and business? Let's embrace the fluidity of our world and turn it into our most significant advantage for RADical success.

Adapt to Thrive

Week 40

REDEFINE INSANITY AND REACH FOR THE SANE: A GUIDE TO STAYING CURRENT IN A CHANGING WORLD

In today's fast-paced world, staying current and adapting to changes in both your personal and professional life are essential. Albert Einstein is widely credited with saying, "The definition of insanity is doing the same thing over and over again and expecting different results." However, in a rapidly evolving climate, doing the same thing in a new environment and expecting the same outcomes is just as insane.

We Can't Stop Change

Change is inevitable, and we risk falling behind if we don't embrace it. Evolution is evident in the technology industry, where companies that were once giants are now obsolete. For example, typewriters and VHS tapes were once the norm, but today they are considered relics. Similarly, with the rise of digital photography, the once-popular photo huts in parking lots are now extinct. These examples serve as metaphors: clinging to old beliefs can lead to irrelevance and obsolescence.

Five Strategies to Stay Current

1. **Research and Pay Attention to Market Trends:** One way to stay current is by keeping a close eye on market trends. Set up alerts and feeds for news related to your local area, hobbies and interests, necessary work skills, and industry news for your business. By doing this, you can anticipate changes and react accordingly.

    According to a 2022 article in Forbes, the top five in-demand skills for the next ten years are digital literacy, data literacy, critical thinking, emotional intelligence, and creativity. [28] If you work in any professional environment, own a business, or manage others, staying updated with the latest trends and technologies is essential to remain competitive.

2. **Embrace New Technology:** Technology constantly evolves, and embracing new technologies can help you work more efficiently and effectively. Social media, for instance, has become a vital communication tool for businesses and individuals. However, it's essential to use your target audience's channels. Trying to use all the available media is not necessarily effective.

    Upgrading your software and hardware regularly or on a schedule can help you take advantage of the latest features and security updates. Setting up automation for tasks you do regularly can save you time and money and reduce errors.

3. **Be Willing to Try New Things:** Trying new things is essential to keep growing and learning. Planning to try something new regularly or creating a bucket list can help you stay motivated and engaged. Seeking new interests, hobbies, and skills can help you remain relevant and adaptable in a rapidly changing environment.

---

[28] https://www.forbes.com/sites/bernardmarr/2022/08/22/the-top-10-most-in-demand-skills-for-the-next-10-years/?sh=1a8d10ca17be

4. **Keep Up Your Education:** Learning new skills is crucial to remain competitive. According to a study conducted by Pew Research, 73% of adults consider themselves lifelong learners. Common characteristics among lifelong learners include knowing their interests, regular goal setting, and the ability to seek resources—all highly successful traits.[29]

   Online learning platforms such as Coursera, Udemy, and edX offer a wide range of courses and certifications to help you learn new skills or improve your existing ones. Many of these courses are free, and some offer certificates upon completion.

5. **Continually Reevaluate Your Methods:** Continually evaluating and fine-tuning your methods can help you work more efficiently and effectively. Making small changes to your work environment or processes can significantly impact productivity. According to a study by Herman Miller, a single change in the work environment can increase productivity by an average of 10%.[30]

Failure to Adapt

One of the most compelling reasons to embrace change and stay current with the latest trends is its impact on your bottom line. For example, consider the case of Blockbuster Video, a company that failed to adapt to changes in the industry and went bankrupt in 2010. At its peak in 2004, Blockbuster had nine thousand stores worldwide and a market capitalization of $5 billion. But by 2010, the company had been overtaken by Netflix, which had embraced the trend toward online streaming and DVD rentals by mail.

---

[29] https://www.pewresearch.org/internet/2016/03/22/lifelong-learning-and-technology/

[30] https://www.hermanmiller.com/content/dam/hermanmiller/documents/research_summaries/wp_MobileWorkers.pdf

Today, Netflix is worth over $250 billion, while Blockbuster is a distant memory.

Another example is Kodak, which was once a giant in the photography industry, with a market capitalization of $31 billion in 1997. However, the company failed to recognize the importance of digital photography and clung to its outdated film-based business model. As a result, it missed out on the digital revolution, and by 2012, the company had filed for bankruptcy.

The lesson here is clear: if you want to succeed in business and life, you must be willing to adapt to changing circumstances and embrace new trends and technologies.

Benefits of Embracing Change

In addition to the financial benefits of staying current, there are also personal benefits. Learning new skills and staying up to date with the latest trends can help you stay engaged and motivated in your work and personal life. It can also help you build new relationships and expand your social network.

In conclusion, the definition of insanity has evolved. Today, the true meaning of insanity is doing the same thing in a new climate and expecting the same results. The world around us is constantly changing, and if we want to succeed, we must be willing to change with it. By embracing new technologies, staying up to date with the latest trends, and continuously learning and growing, we can become more successful, fulfilled, and, ultimately, sane.

Action: Conduct a Personal Innovation Audit

Let's transform our approach to change and innovation! Your mission, should you accept it, involves a simple but powerful exercise: a personal innovation audit.

1. **Reflect on Your Current Practices:** Take a moment to jot down the critical aspects of your work or personal life. How do you approach tasks? What technologies or methods do you rely on?
2. **Identify Potential for Change:** Look at each area you've listed. Where could new trends, technologies, or strategies be implemented? Are you clinging to outdated practices that could be hindering your growth?
3. **Research Trends:** Research the latest trends or technologies for each area identified. Use resources like industry publications, online courses, or even YouTube tutorials to educate yourself about new possibilities.
4. **Create an Action Plan:** Draft a simple action plan based on your research. It could be as straightforward as trying a new software tool, enrolling in an online course, or networking with professionals in your field to gain insights.
5. **Implement and Review Changes:** Start implementing these changes, no matter how small. Regularly review their impact on your efficiency, effectiveness, and satisfaction.

Remember, as we say at RAD Strategic Partners, embracing change isn't just about keeping up—it's about leading the way. By regularly auditing and updating your methods and mindset, you're not just adapting to change but harnessing it for RADical success.

Week 41

PRACTICE GRATITUDE: CREATE ABUNDANCE WITH A SIMPLE PRACTICE

The Power of Gratitude: More Than Just a Trend

Gratitude isn't just a buzzword in the self-help industry—it's a profound practice that can transform our lives. The concept of expressing thanks and appreciating what we have, rather than focusing on what we lack, is a timeless piece of wisdom. It's not just about feeling good; gratitude brings tangible benefits to our lives.

Reticular Activating System (RAS): The Brain's Filter

Our brain's reticular activating system (RAS) is crucial in how we perceive the world. It filters the immense amount of information we encounter daily, highlighting what aligns with our focus. When we cultivate gratitude, we tune our RAS to notice more positivity, enhancing our perception of life's blessings.

Expressing Gratitude: A Ripple Effect

Acknowledging the good in others and expressing our gratitude doesn't just make them feel valued—it also influences their behavior positively. This can be particularly impactful in professional settings. When you express genuine appreciation, it not only strengthens your relationships but can also help chart a more successful career path and foster a collaborative work environment.

Gratitude's Broader Impact

Focusing on negative aspects can inadvertently attract more of the same. Hence, shifting your focus to gratitude can have a profound impact. Studies consistently show the benefits of gratitude, including improved relationships, better physical and mental health, and even enhanced sleep quality.[31] Grateful individuals often engage in healthier behaviors, experience fewer toxic emotions, and maintain a generally happier outlook.

Building Resilience through Gratitude

The practice of gratitude is influential in overcoming trauma and building resilience. By reducing the tendency to engage in unfavorable social comparisons, gratitude helps bolster self-esteem and mental strength—critical factors in coping with challenging life events.

Reducing Aggression and Enhancing Empathy

Gratitude isn't just about feeling good, it also plays a role in how we interact with others. It can reduce aggressive behavior and enhance our capacity for empathy, making our social interactions more positive and fulfilling.

Practical Steps to Cultivate Gratitude

Creating abundance through gratitude starts with a personal practice. It can be as simple as taking a moment each day to

---

[31] There are many. Here is one from UCLA https://www.uclahealth. org/news/article/health-benefits-gratitude#:~:text=Research%20 shows%20that%20practicing%20gratitude,positively%20affect%20 your%20physical%20health.

acknowledge the beauty and positives in life. Gratitude might include appreciating supportive relationships, valuing your work environment, or marveling at the wonders of nature and technology.

Expressing Gratitude for Greater Success

Going beyond internal gratitude, expressing it outwardly can significantly amplify your success. Whether it's thanking customers, acknowledging a colleague's help, or simply showing appreciation in your daily interactions, expressing gratitude can deepen connections and open doors to new opportunities.

Actionable Strategies for Gratitude

- **Begin with a Simple "Thank You":** Start your gratitude practice with the easy act of saying thanks. This fundamental expression of appreciation can profoundly impact your relationships and interactions.
- **Leverage Technology for Gratitude:** Use autoresponders or other digital tools to thank customers or colleagues; adding a personal touch to your professional interactions.
- **Personalized Appreciation:** Consider sending handwritten thank-you notes or customized messages. Such gestures can significantly strengthen your relationships and build a network of mutual support and respect.

Gratitude as a Path to Success

Embracing gratitude in personal and professional aspects of life is more than just a practice; it's a pathway to success. It shapes how we see the world, interact with others, and respond to life's challenges. By integrating gratitude into our daily routine and making it a habit to express it genuinely, we pave the way for a more fulfilling, successful, and abundant life. Recognizing and appreciating the good around us opens us to even greater possibilities and achievements.

Action Steps: Cultivating Gratitude for Abundance

Start Your Gratitude Journal

- **Action Item:** Begin a gratitude journal today. Each evening, jot down three things you were grateful for during the day. These can range from significant achievements to simple joys like a sunny day or a good cup of coffee. This simple act refocuses your RAS on the positives, creating a more appreciative mindset.

Express Gratitude to Others

- **Action Item:** Identify one person each week who has positively impacted your life or work. Reach out to them with a thank-you note, an email, or a phone call. Make this expression of gratitude specific to what they've done and how it affected you. Notice the change in your relationship and the positivity it brings.

Gratitude in Challenges

- **Action Item:** When faced with a challenging situation or a "lemon," instead of reacting with frustration, pause and identify a learning or positive aspect of this challenge. How can this experience enrich your growth or understanding?

Why do this? At RAD Strategic Partners, we know that gratitude isn't just a feel-good exercise—it's a powerful tool for creating abundance in your life. By recognizing the good in your life and expressing gratitude to others, you improve your mental and emotional well-being, foster positive relationships, and open yourself up to new opportunities and successes. It's about shifting your focus to abundance and maximizing what you have.

Week 42

EMBRACE CHANGE: FREE YOURSELF FROM OUTDATED IDEAS AND BELIEFS

It has been said that it is easier for companies to come up with new ideas than to let go of old ones. This concept applies not only to businesses but also to individuals striving to achieve their goals and dreams. Often, outdated ideas and beliefs hinder progress. In this chapter, we will explore the difference between ideas and beliefs, uncover common false beliefs, and discover ways to identify and release beliefs that hold us back.

Beliefs and ideas are similar but not the same, and our beliefs often prevent us from fully exploring and implementing new ideas. Beliefs are deeply held convictions we accept as accurate, while ideas are mental constructs or concepts that can lead to new perspectives, solutions, or actions. Beliefs are more stable and influential, shaping our worldview, while ideas are more fluid and serve as catalysts for innovation and growth.

Unmasking Outdated Beliefs

Beliefs differ from ideas as they are deeply ingrained and accepted as unalterable truths. However, we can change our beliefs, and it is essential to assess their accuracy. Let's debunk a few widely accepted false statements: we use only 10% of our brains, George Washington had wooden teeth, witches were burned at the stake in Salem, eight glasses of water are necessary daily, a twenty-four-hour wait is mandatory to file a missing person report, and sugar causes hyperactivity in children. These examples are commonly held beliefs, and none are accurate. They demonstrate how easily false beliefs can take root.

Unearthing Limiting Beliefs

Examining our beliefs and determining which ones impede our progress is crucial. To identify them, reflect on our routines, procedures, excuses, and environment. Are we clinging to outdated tools or methods simply because they are familiar? Challenging our beliefs involves seeking ways to upgrade, optimize, and improve functionality. Embrace new shortcuts and life hacks that can enhance our efficiency and effectiveness.

Learning from Past Experiences

Resistance to ideas often stems from previous unsuccessful attempts. However, it is essential to consider whether the timing was right, the skills were lacking, or the message needed to be refined. Rather than dismissing ideas outright, explore minor tweaks or adjustments that could make a significant difference. Learning from failure is valuable, but being open to revisiting ideas is equally important.

Reevaluating Core Beliefs

Core beliefs shape our identity and influence our actions. They are deeply ingrained thoughts such as "I am..." or "the world is..." It is crucial to challenge these beliefs to achieve our goals. Recognize that changing core beliefs will lead to changed actions. Regularly examining and consciously choosing our beliefs allows us to adapt and evolve, ensuring personal growth and success.

Finding Outdated Beliefs

Look in these places for ideas and beliefs that may be past their time:

1. What have you resisted upgrading or changing because your version is good enough? Many, though certainly not all, upgrades significantly improve functionality. We get stuck in the habit of not wanting to learn a new tool without understanding the time and effort it will save us in the future.

2. What systems and procedures do you regularly follow without considering whether that may be the best way to achieve your aim because "that is how they are done"? It's great to learn new shortcuts. They enhance our lives with minimal discomfort. Think of a life hack you discovered that delighted you and seek out more.

3. What ideas have you resisted because you tried them before, and they did not work, yet others seem to be having success with them? What technology have you shied away from because you tested an early version that wasn't quite right then?

4. Think back to a core belief you held for a long time before discovering it was untrue. Perhaps it's something you were taught to believe or learned from previous experience. Review your beliefs and determine which might be worth letting go or might require exploring additional viewpoints.

Overcoming the resistance to change and letting go of outdated ideas and beliefs is a transformative process. By recognizing the distinction between ideas and beliefs, questioning the accuracy of our beliefs, unmasking false statements, and reevaluating core beliefs, we can break free from the limitations that hold us back. Embrace the discomfort of change, adapt to the evolving world, and unlock your potential for RADical success.

Embrace Change: Action for RADical Success

Ready to break free from outdated beliefs and ideas? Your mission is to embark on a journey of self-reflection and change. Here's how:

1. **Identify and Challenge a Core Belief:** Select one belief you've held for a long time. It could be a belief about your capabilities, the world, or how things should be done. Ask yourself, "Is this belief still serving my purpose? Could there be another perspective I haven't considered?"

2. **Journal Your Thoughts:** Write down this belief and how it has influenced your decisions and actions in the past. Reflect on situations where this belief might have held you back.

3. **Seek Alternative Viewpoints:** Look for information, opinions, or experiences that challenge your belief. This could involve reading articles, listening to podcasts, or conversing with people with different viewpoints.

4. **Create a New Belief Statement:** Based on your new insights, craft a belief statement that better aligns with your current goals and aspirations. For example, if your old belief was "I'm not good at adapting to new technology," your new belief could be "I am capable of learning and utilizing new technology effectively."

5. **Put It into Practice:** Live according to your new belief for the next month. Observe the changes in your attitude, approach to challenges, and the outcomes of your actions.

As we say at RAD Strategic Partners, letting go of outdated beliefs opens doors to new opportunities and growth. By consciously choosing our beliefs and challenging the old ones, we pave the way for innovation, adaptation, and RADical success. Start today and witness the transformation in your personal and professional life. Remember, the power to change lies within you!

Week 43

CONQUER YOUR INNER VICTIM: UNLEASHING THE VICTOR WITHIN YOU FOR SUCCESS

Are you a victor or a victim? This isn't merely a rhetorical question; it's a reflection of your mindset, which in turn shapes your reality—in both life and business. While it's tempting to adopt a victim mentality due to uncontrollable events and challenges, that choice often leaves us feeling powerless and unfulfilled. In contrast, choosing to be a victor makes us proactive, resilient, and ultimately more successful. Your daily choice between these two mindsets can be pivotal in your journey toward achieving your goals.

The Psychology of the Victim vs. The Victor

The Victim Mindset

Victims see the world as an uncontrollable, chaotic place where things happen to them. Their inner monologue often includes blame and excuses: the economy is terrible, competitors are too strong, or we didn't get the right opportunities. A study by the American Psychological Association found that individuals who adopt a victim mentality are more likely to suffer from stress and depression.[32]

---

[32] Zur, O., "The Psychology of Victimhood," In R. H. Wright & N. A. Cummings (Eds.), *Destructive trends in mental health: The well-intentioned path to harm* , (Imprint Routledge, 2005), pp. 45-64: Routledge

The Victor Mindset

Victors, on the other hand, understand that they can influence outcomes through their actions. Even in the toughest of times, they find a way to turn lemons into lemonade. They embrace challenges as opportunities for growth. A study published in the Journal of Managerial Psychology states that a proactive mindset correlates strongly with career success and general well-being.[33]

The Dichotomy Within You

It's almost as if we have two selves within us—the victim and the victor. While the victim within us blames circumstances, the victor takes control. Every day, we decide which version gets to lead.

Stop Blaming; Start Acting

One of the crucial steps to conquering your inner victim is to stop blaming external circumstances. Instead, focus on actionable solutions. Victor-minded individuals don't just complain about an empty store; they strategize and innovate to attract customers. They own their actions and outcomes.

Taking Responsibility—A Case Study

Years ago, my son found himself alone and injured. Lying there, he could've easily slipped into victimhood, waiting for someone to rescue him. However, he realized no one was coming; he had to save himself. Picking himself up, he called for advice on treating his scraped knee. The lesson here? We're all ultimately responsible for our fate. The sooner we realize this, the sooner we can act to improve our circumstances.

---

[33] Yang, Fu & Chau, Rebecca, "Proactive personality and career success," *Journal of managerial psychology,* Vol. 31, Issue 2, pages 467 – 482.

Turning Challenges into Opportunities

When unexpected events disrupt our plans, a victor's mentality helps us adapt and pivot rather than wallow in self-pity. An unforeseen obstacle becomes an opportunity to innovate. A sudden market downturn becomes a chance to refine our business strategies.

Accountability and Results

Victors know that success comes from a combination of planning, action, and adaptability. They understand the value of holding themselves accountable, no matter the external circumstances. When things don't go as planned, they revise their strategy and try again.

Embrace the Victor Within

When we conquer our inner victim, we grant ourselves the power to shape our destiny. It's more than just positive thinking; it's a fundamental shift in how we approach life's challenges and opportunities. As the saying goes, "Life is 10% what happens to us and 90% how we react to it."

Take Action Today

- Conduct a self-audit to identify areas where a victim mentality is holding you back.
- Make a list of challenges you face and brainstorm actionable solutions.
- Hold yourself accountable. Set measurable goals and commit to achieving them.

In summary, the path to success starts from within. By transforming your mindset from a victim to a victor, you're not just changing your thought patterns but your life. Make the choice today—and every day—to conquer your inner victim and let your inner victor rise and shine.

Your Next Step to Unleashing the Victor Within

You're inspired and ready to kick that inner victim to the curb. So, what's the immediate next action item you can take?

Action Item: Identify a recent challenge or obstacle you've faced that triggered your "victim" mindset. Write it down. Next to it, list three proactive steps you could take to turn that situation into an opportunity for growth or improvement.

Why This Works: Why are we focusing on this? At RAD Strategic Partners, we believe awareness is the first step in transformation. Pinpointing the challenges that trigger your victim mentality can help you understand the thought patterns you need to change. But we don't stop at mere awareness. You're taking that newfound understanding and turning it into a strategic action plan for your RADical success journey by identifying specific, actionable steps.

So go ahead, make that shift from victim to victor, and let your inner conqueror rise and shine!

Month 11

PRACTICAL TACTICS

Navigating the Tactical Terrain: Practical Tools for RADical Success

Welcome to month eleven, where we delve into the nitty-gritty, the essential tactical stuff that often decides the fate of our business and personal aspirations. This section is about equipping you with practical, tangible tools and strategies to navigate the often unpredictable waters of life and business.

First up, we tackle how to avoid dips in business. Here, we'll explore proactive strategies to anticipate, mitigate, and recover from downturns. It's about building resilience and adaptability into the very fabric of your business model.

Preparing for anything isn't just sage advice; it's a survival skill in today's fast-paced world. We'll discuss the art of foresight and planning, ensuring you're always a step ahead, no matter what life throws your way.

Mastering cash flow is next on our agenda. Understanding and optimizing cash flow is crucial whether you're running a multinational corporation or managing your household finances. We'll break down complex financial concepts into clear, actionable steps.

Building a solid reputation is your social currency in the business world. We'll guide you on crafting and maintaining a reputation that opens doors, attracts opportunities, and establishes trust.

Finally, funding your dreams goes beyond traditional financial advice. It's about creative and practical ways to secure the necessary resources to bring your visions to life.

Ready to dive into the tactical toolkit for RADical success? Let's sharpen those skills and give you the know-how to thrive in any scenario.

Tactical Tool Kit

Week 44

AVOID VALLEYS AND MAINTAIN BUSINESS GROWTH: SUSTAINING MOMENTUM AND AVOIDING DOWNTURNS

In the ever-changing business landscape, it's not uncommon for entrepreneurs, sales professionals, and executives to experience fluctuations in their customer base and business revenue. One moment, we find ourselves overwhelmed with an abundance of work, and the next, we're left wondering where all the business went. This unpredictable cycle results from a common pitfall: neglecting marketing and prospecting efforts during busy periods. To ensure sustainable growth, we must understand the sales cycle, streamline lead generation, optimize conversion rates, and effectively manage workflow and client expectations. Here we'll delve into these essential steps to help you maintain consistent business growth.

Five Steps to Avoid Valleys and Maintain Consistent Business Growth

1. **Understanding the Sales Cycle**

   We must comprehend our sales cycle thoroughly to prevent the adverse effects of a sudden drop in business. This cycle encompasses the time from initial prospect identification to receiving payment for our products or services. Different industries and businesses have varying sales cycles, and neglecting prospecting during any phase can leave us without revenue months in the future. For instance, if our sales cycle typically spans six months, failing to prospect in May means we won't see any income in November. As sales cycles lengthen, keeping our pipeline active becomes even more critical, ensuring a steady flow of prospects ready to convert when we need them.

2. **Quantifying Our Efforts**

To effectively manage our marketing and prospecting activities, it's essential to quantify our efforts through data analysis. We can create a proactive marketing plan that aligns with our revenue goals by doing simple math and understanding the numbers behind our customer acquisition process. Start by determining how many customers are needed to reach your desired revenue target. Track your conversion rate over time to calculate how many prospects you need to engage to achieve that desired customer count. Furthermore, measure the results of various marketing channels to identify which strategies yield the most promising outcomes, helping you allocate resources more efficiently.

3. **Marketing and Prospecting Consistently**

One of the most common mistakes businesses make when experiencing a surge in work is reducing or completely halting our marketing and prospecting efforts. While it may seem counterintuitive, maintaining a consistent level of marketing is crucial even during busy times. Automating certain aspects of our marketing process can help ensure our efforts remain consistent. By increasing or decreasing the intensity of our marketing efforts based on business demands, we can adapt to fluctuating workloads without compromising the future growth of our business.

4. **Managing Expectations and Scheduling**

   It is crucial for businesses that handle large projects with long sales cycles to manage expectations effectively. Limited capacity to handle many clients at once necessitates careful scheduling and clear communication with prospects. Avoid overpromising and underdelivering by assessing your ability and setting realistic timelines and deliverables. By proactively managing client expectations, you can maintain a positive reputation, secure future projects, and ensure client satisfaction.

5. **Maintaining Activity Levels**

   Once we have determined the necessary marketing and prospecting activities to achieve our revenue goals, we must schedule dedicated time for these tasks and stick to them. Treat marketing and prospecting as nonnegotiable activities, even during your busiest periods. Prioritize them alongside client work, and allocate time and resources accordingly. If you find that you cannot keep up with the necessary marketing and prospecting efforts, it's a clear indication that you won't reach your revenue goals unless you make some adjustments. In such cases, consider outsourcing certain activities to maintain the desired pace.

Consistent business growth requires a strategic approach encompassing understanding the sales cycle, quantifying marketing efforts, maintaining constant activity levels, and managing client expectations. We can ensure a steady flow of leads and prospects by continuously prospecting, measuring conversion rates, and aligning marketing strategies with revenue goals. Remember, even during busy periods, it is crucial to maintain marketing efforts and avoid the pitfalls of feast and famine. By effectively managing expectations and delivering on commitments, we can secure a positive reputation and foster long-term success for our business. Stay proactive, keep the numbers in mind, and dedicate time to marketing and prospecting to sustain growth and thrive in a competitive marketplace.

Action Item: Sustaining Growth through Consistency

1. **Sales Cycle Examination:** Pull out your business diary and map out your typical sales cycle. From lead generation to final sale, note the average time each phase takes. Label this your "cycle map."
2. **Quantify to Qualify:** Grab a calculator and crunch some numbers. How many customers do you need to meet your revenue target? What's your current conversion rate? Use this data to determine how many prospects you must regularly engage with. We're talking serious number crunching here.
3. **Marketing Consistency Plan:** Even if you're up to your neck in work, marketing can't take a backseat. Schedule a regular marketing hour each week (yes, even when you're swamped) to keep your efforts humming. This is your consistent marketing momentum.
4. **Expectation Management Schedule:** Set aside weekly time to review project timelines and communicate with clients. This is your expectation alignment time. Clear communication through a quick call or an email is your secret weapon.
5. **Activity Level Audit:** Review your marketing and prospecting activities at the end of each month. Are they aligned with your set goals? If not, consider outsourcing to keep the momentum. This is your growth gauge.

At RAD Strategic Partners, we understand that consistent effort beats occasional brilliance. By following these steps, you're not just avoiding valleys but building mountains of success. Think of it as your business's fitness routine—it's all about maintaining that growth muscle.

Week 45

PREPARE FOR ANYTHING: SEVEN ESSENTIAL STEPS TO TAKE

Recent events have shown us that anything can happen in the world. I could have written that sentence any time in the past twenty years, and it would be correct! New inventions, wars, pandemics, wild weather, corrupt leaders disrupting governments, shortages, surpluses, and more have occurred in recent decades. It's hard to pretend the world is predictable when it continually teaches us otherwise.

We can never predict the future, but we can control how we respond. By being prepared for any situation in our business, career, and life, we can weather any storm, even those we could not have foreseen. Today, we will discuss seven essential steps to take to prepare for anything.

1. **Communications**
   Communication is critical in any emergency. We must have reliable communication with our team, family, clients, and peers if an emergency arises. It is crucial to have a backup plan in case the primary mode of communication fails. For example, if the cell phone network goes down, is there a landline or a two-way radio as an alternative means of communication? If our team is in different locations, can we use a messaging app or video conferencing tool to stay connected?

2. **Physical Space**

   If our physical space becomes compromised due to an emergency, we need a backup plan to ensure our operations can continue. For example, if we have a brick-and-mortar store, we may need to evacuate or close temporarily due to a natural disaster. In such cases, it is essential to have a contingency plan, such as working from home or finding a temporary location to operate from. We should also ensure that our team has the tools and resources to work remotely, such as laptops, internet access, and software applications.

3. **Data**

   In today's digital age, data is the lifeblood of many businesses. Losing critical data due to a cyberattack, natural disaster, or hardware failure can be devastating. Ensuring our essential records are safe, secure, and backed up is critical. Cloud-based storage solutions such as Google Drive, Dropbox, and OneDrive offer affordable and convenient ways to back up our data. We can also consider using a secure external hard drive or a tape backup system. This is true of our personal records as well as our business records.

4. **Teams**

   Our team may be our employees, peers, family, or support network. In an emergency, we must have a plan to ensure our team can carry on without us. We should create an accessible checklist of critical information our team would need to carry on in our absence, such as contact information for clients, vendors, and suppliers; passwords for critical systems, and instructions for essential processes. We should also designate a backup person to take over our responsibilities if we are suddenly unable to do so. This is true of our home responsibilities as well.

5. **Insurance**

   Insurance is a critical component of any disaster preparedness plan. It can help protect us against financial losses from damage to our physical space, equipment, inventory, or other assets. We should ensure that we have adequate insurance coverage for our business or personal property and review our policy regularly to ensure that it meets our evolving needs. We should also consider purchasing business interruption insurance to cover lost income and expenses if we cannot operate due to an emergency.

6. **Cash**

   In an emergency, cash is king. We need to have some emergency cash on hand that we can use to continue operations in the event of a power outage or other banking disruption. While digital payment methods such as credit cards, PayPal, and Venmo are convenient, they may not be available during a crisis. We should also consider a backup funding source, such as a business line of credit or a personal emergency fund, to help us cover unexpected expenses.

7. **Systems**

   Our systems are the backbone of our business. If they fail, our operations may come to a standstill, leading to lost revenue, productivity, and customer complaints. Having reliable systems ensures our business can continue operating in an emergency. These include our computers, phones, and other technology we rely on for daily operations. We need backups for all critical systems, including redundant power supplies, backup generators, and backup internet connections.

Remember, preparation is key to maintaining control over our inside world when everything else is outside of our control. By preparing now, we can ensure we are ready to weather any storm and come out stronger on the other side.

We can't control the world around us, but we can control our response. We need not be ships in the sea tossed about every time there is a storm if we prepare to continue with our goals, lives, and businesses no matter what.

In conclusion, being prepared for anything is a catchy phrase and a necessary mindset in today's unpredictable world. By following the tips and suggestions outlined here, we can start preparing for any potential emergency, disaster, or unexpected event that might occur in our personal or professional lives.

Being prepared for any eventuality includes having a solid financial strategy. Managing cash flow effectively ensures we have the resources to navigate unforeseen challenges and maintain stability in our business.

Disaster Plan Checklist

Action Item: Choose Your Preparation Pillar

1. **Select Your Focus Area:** Review the seven essential steps and pick one area that resonates most or is most relevant to you.
2. **Conduct a Deep Dive Assessment:** Once you've chosen your focus area, it's time to conduct a thorough assessment. For example, evaluate your current data backup and security measures if you decide to focus on data. Are they robust enough?
3. **Create a Contingency Plan:** Develop a comprehensive contingency plan for your chosen area based on your assessment. This plan should cover worst-case scenarios.
4. **Allocate Resources:** Determine what resources (time, money, personnel) you'll need to implement and maintain your plan. This step is all about turning plans into action.
5. **Train Your Team:** If your plan involves other team members, make sure they are aware of the plan and trained on it. This might mean running drills on alternative communication methods if your focus is communication.
6. **Review and Update Regularly:** Mark your calendar for a periodic review of this plan. The world changes rapidly, and so should your preparations. Adjust and refine as necessary.
7. **Choose an Accountability Buddy:** Share your plan with a trusted colleague, mentor, or peer.

Why are we doing this? Being prepared isn't just about having a plan but a dynamic strategy that evolves with changing circumstances. By focusing on one area at a time, you're not just preparing for the unexpected but building a resilient foundation for continuous success.

Week 46

MONEY TALKS: MASTERING THE DANCE OF CASH FLOW

Profit may be nice, but like we said in the previous chapter: cash is the true king. You can't buy groceries with paper profits. So, how's your cash flow dance going? Are you two-stepping to financial success or tripping over your shoelaces? Fear not! We're here to help you move toward a flourishing business and a fulfilling life. Let's get serious about generating cash flow.

Ten Ways to Improve Your Cash Flow

1. **Invoice Ninja Moves:** Don't let your invoices gather dust like a forgotten dance partner. Whip out those invoices with the speed of a ninja! Send them faster than a squirrel chasing a nut. The quicker they're out, the faster you'll hear the sweet sound of cash flowing into your pocket.
2. **The Power of Advance Payments:** Picture this: a customer waltzing in and paying upfront, like a knight in shining armor. Offer discounts or exclusive perks for those gallant souls who pay in advance. Your cash flow will rise like a crescendo, and you'll feel like a financial maestro.
3. **Cash Flow Party Crashers:** Keep an eagle eye on your expenses; those sneaky party crashers can wreak havoc on your cash flow fiesta. Slice and dice your costs like a master

sushi chef. Trim the excess fat, and you'll dance to a leaner financial tune.

4. **Quick Payments Hustle:** Don't be shy; it's time to put on your cash flow hustle! Reach out to slow-paying customers like a smooth-talking detective. Remind them politely but firmly that the time to pay is now. Watch how the rhythm of cash picks up its pace.

5. **Painless Payment Terms:** Negotiate those payment terms like a seasoned diplomat. Find a harmony that suits both parties. You want to avoid a cash flow tango with terms that leave you stumbling and twirling. Remember, a fair deal leads to a long-lasting partnership.

6. **Dazzling Discounts (For Early Birds):** Entice your customers with discounts that sparkle like a disco ball. A little discount can go a long way in bringing those payments to your doorstep. They'll feel like they've discovered the dance floor deal of the century.

7. **Budget Boogie Nights:** Create a budget as tight as a pair of disco pants. Track your cash flow precisely, and you'll know where every dollar shakes its groove. It's like a dance choreography that keeps your finances on track.

8. **Diversified Dance Partners:** Relying on one big client can be as risky as doing the tango on roller skates. Expand your clientele like a social butterfly, and you'll have a diverse pool of partners, keeping your cash flow waltzing gracefully.

9. **Cash Reserves, the Safety Dance:** Picture this: you're in the middle of a cash flow conga, and suddenly, a financial emergency strikes. Fear not! With a healthy cash reserve, you can keep the dance floor moving and grooving, even during tough times.

10. **The Cash Flow Forecast Jive:** Master the art of forecasting like a meteorologist on steroids. Predict the cash flow climate and plan your moves accordingly. With a crystal ball for your finances, you'll dance confidently into the future.

Remember, my fellow cash flow maestros, managing your cash flow is like leading a dance—it requires finesse, planning, and a sprinkle of charisma. Embrace these tips, and you'll be the Fred Astaire of cash flow in no time, tapping your way to financial success and making your business dreams come true!

We know you can't implement all these moves at once, but remember, Rome wasn't built in a day, and even Michael Jackson had to practice his moonwalk. Take your time, introduce these tips one by one, and before you know it, you'll be doing the cash flow cha-cha with ease.

Strong cash flow leads to a strong business. It's like a dance that needs constant practice and fine-tuning. Don't let unexpected bills or sudden expenses take the lead. With proper planning and forecasting, you'll master your financial dance floor.

So, Let's Recap

Embrace the cash-generating mindset, keep an eye on your cash outflow, and never forget the power of a well-managed cash flow forecast. Sales may bring the rhythm, but it's the proper planning and execution that will keep the party going.

Remember, if you can't forecast your next month's sales and expenses, you might as well be doing the cha-cha in the dark! So, put on your cash flow dancing shoes, step out confidently, and watch your business thrive like never before. Let those dollars do the talking; soon enough, you'll be living your dreams. Cha-ching!

Action Item: Cash Flow Choreography—Choose One from the List Below

1. **Invoice Timing Tango:** Look at your current invoicing process. Set a goal for the next month to reduce your invoice issue time by half.
2. **Advance Payment Waltz:** Identify one service or product you can offer with an advance payment option. Introduce an incentive for those early birds.
3. **Expense Salsa:** Go through your expenses and identify at least one area you can trim. Maybe it's that subscription you rarely use.
4. **Payment Terms Rumba:** Revisit your payment terms with one of your clients or suppliers. Negotiate terms that improve your cash flow rhythm.
5. **Disco Discounts:** Plan a promotion offering a small discount for early payments. Make it as dazzling as a disco ball, something your clients can't resist.
6. **Budget Boogie:** If you don't have a budget, now's the time to create one. If you have one, it's time for a review.
7. **Clientele Conga Line:** Look at your client list. Is there too much reliance on a few? Set a goal to bring in at least two new clients next month.
8. **Cash Reserve Shuffle:** Assess your current cash reserves. Are they sufficient? Set a target to increase this by a certain percentage over the next quarter.
9. **Forecast Foxtrot:** Get into the habit of forecasting your cash flow. Start with next month.

Why are we doing this? Mastering the cash flow dance isn't about nailing one big move. It's about learning a series of small steps that, when put together, create a beautifully choreographed financial success story.

Week 47

BUILD A STRONG REPUTATION: UNLOCKING SUCCESS AND TRUST

In today's competitive business landscape, establishing and nurturing a solid reputation is paramount to achieving long-term success. Your reputation serves as a foundation for trust, credibility, and opportunities. Just as Leo Durocher's famous quote, "Nice guys finish last," has been debunked, it is evident that individuals with a positive reputation ultimately finish first. In this chapter, we will explore the importance of building a strong reputation, delve into the perception-reality dynamic, and provide practical steps to enhance and safeguard your reputation.

The Power of Reputation

Your reputation holds immense power in shaping the growth and prosperity of your business. Consider the following: Would you willingly engage in business with someone whose reputation you don't trust? How often do you base your decisions on the reputation of others? These questions emphasize reputation's critical role in our personal and professional lives. A strong reputation attracts potential clients, customers, and partners; fosters loyalty; and opens doors to new opportunities.

Perception: The Key to Reputation

Often touted as reality, perception dramatically influences how others perceive and evaluate you. It is crucial to gain insight into how people perceive you in order to mold and manage your reputation effectively. Start by reflecting on the following questions:

1. How do people you know perceive you?
2. How do new introductions react to you?
3. Are you viewed as competent and knowledgeable in your field?
4. Are you perceived as a giver or a taker?
5. Do others believe you have a strong network?
6. Are you well-liked by your peers? Are you considered a person of integrity?
7. Do people value and respect your opinion?
8. Are you honest and sincere in your interactions?
9. Do you consistently follow through on your commitments?
10. Do you exhibit leadership qualities without being overbearing or overanxious?

By honestly answering these questions, you can identify areas for improvement and take proactive steps to enhance your reputation.

Practical Steps to Building a Strong Reputation

1. **Self-Reflection:** Begin by conducting an honest self-assessment. Identify your strengths and areas for growth. Acknowledge any behaviors or actions that may hinder the development of a strong reputation.
2. **Constructive Criticism:** Actively seek feedback from trusted colleagues, mentors, and friends. Encourage them to provide constructive criticism and highlight areas where you may be falling short. Embrace their perspectives as valuable opportunities for self-improvement.

3. **Feedback Implementation:** Take concrete steps to address the feedback you receive. Implement changes that align with your desired reputation and work on developing skills or qualities that will positively impact how others perceive you.

4. **Consistency:** Consistency is critical to building a solid reputation. Ensure that your words and actions align consistently with your desired reputation. Be reliable, follow through on commitments, and maintain integrity in all interactions.

5. **Networking:** Cultivate a robust network of contacts who can vouch for your credibility and expertise. Actively engage in professional associations, attend industry events, and seek opportunities to collaborate with others. Building genuine relationships will contribute to your reputation as a well-connected individual.

6. **Thought Leadership:** Establish yourself as an expert in your field by sharing your knowledge and insights. Contribute to industry publications, speak at conferences, or create content through blogs or social media platforms. Demonstrating expertise enhances your reputation as a knowledgeable professional.

7. **Effective Communication:** Master the art of effective communication. Listen actively, articulate your thoughts clearly, and adapt your communication style to suit different audiences. This skill fosters respect, understanding, and trust, contributing to a positive reputation.

8. **Personal Branding:** Develop a strong personal brand that reflects your values, expertise, and unique qualities. Consistently present yourself professionally, both online and offline. Craft a compelling personal narrative that highlights your achievements and strengths.

9. **Generosity:** Cultivate a reputation as a giver rather than a taker. Offer support, mentorship, and assistance to others. Actively contribute to your community and industry, and seek opportunities to help others succeed. Generosity and selflessness create a lasting positive impression.

10. **Continuous Improvement:** Never stop growing and learning. Invest in your professional development, stay updated with industry trends, and embrace new technologies. Demonstrating a commitment to growth and improvement reinforces your reputation as a competent and adaptable professional.

Building a strong reputation is more vital than ever in today's interconnected world. Your reputation serves as a currency of trust, opening doors to new opportunities and fostering long-term success. By understanding the power of perception, engaging in self-reflection, seeking feedback, and implementing the practical steps outlined above, you can cultivate a reputation that resonates with integrity, expertise, and credibility. Remember, your reputation is a priceless asset—nurture, protect, and let it guide you toward a fulfilling and prosperous future.

Action Item: Crafting Your Reputation Masterpiece—Choose One

1. **Feedback Gallery Walk:** Reach out to at least three people you trust—a mix of colleagues, mentors, and friends. Ask for their candid feedback on your professional reputation.
2. **Action Plan Sculpture:** Carve out an action plan based on the feedback. Identify one key area you want to improve and set a specific, achievable goal for the next month.
3. **Networking Mosaic:** Plan to attend one networking event or engage in one networking activity this month.
4. **Thought Leadership Gallery:** Write one blog post, article, or LinkedIn post sharing your expertise or insights.
5. **Communication Workshop:** For one week, consciously enhance one aspect of your communication skills. It could be active listening, clarity in conveying your thoughts, or tailoring your message to your audience.
6. **Personal Brand Exhibit:** Review your online presence (LinkedIn, personal website, etc.) and ensure it aligns with the personal brand you want to project.
7. **The Giver's Fair:** Identify one opportunity to give back this month.
8. **Continuous Learning Journey:** Enroll in a webinar, workshop, or course related to your field.

Why are we doing this? A strong reputation is like a masterpiece—crafted with patience, skill, and authenticity over time. By taking these steps, you're not just painting a picture of success; you're creating a legacy of trust and credibility.

Week 48

THE MEANS OF EXCHANGE: HOW WE CREATE THE PATHWAY TO OUR DREAMS

In the grand theater of life and business, the currency that fuels dreams is exchange. It's the balance of giving and taking, crafting and creating, knowing and growing. It's not just about money. It's about the dreams that fuel our daily lives and the steps we take to make them come true.

Money as a Measure

In our complex world, we need something to keep things even, to balance supply with demand. Money is often viewed as the goal, but what if I told you that it's merely a measure? It's the ticket to your dreams.

Imagine your most significant aspirations. Perhaps you want to build a multimillion-dollar business or help feed a town—maybe both! Whether you want to surf all day or raise a family, you need the goods and services of others to achieve those things. The magic of realizing these dreams lies in the cash flow you generate.

Dreaming Big and Beyond

Your potential to dream expands with the ability to harness resources. So, dream big, and then find ideas to generate those resources.

Have you considered your capital requirements? It's an early step in success, understanding what's required to do everything you desire. Cash is indeed king, both in business and in life.

What's on your wish list? Make that list of everything you desire, as if money were no object. Then ask yourself, do you have enough revenue in place to achieve that list? If not, it's time to employ some cash flow strategies.

The Five-Act Play to Success

1. **Do Your Math:** What's your dream's price tag? Analyze your needs, desires, and costs across various time frames, from daily to annual budgets.
2. **Forecast Revenue:** Project your revenue not only for the upcoming year but five years ahead. Look into market trends, anticipate changes, and be prepared.
3. **Close the Gap:** Identify the difference between your current status and where you want to be. Develop strategies to bridge this gap, and don't be afraid to seek professional advice if needed.
4. **See Yourself Living Your Dream:** Release the inner brakes by visualizing success. Let your dreams be the blueprints of your reality. Daily reflections on this vision will nourish your determination.
5. **Take Action:** Dreams demand execution. Make it happen, one step at a time. Engage in a consistent effort, seek feedback, and be prepared to make course corrections.

The Power of Belief and Visualization

The words of Henry Ford ring true: "Whether you think you can, or you think you can't—you're right." Your vision of success starts in your mind. Believe in your ability, and the cash flow strategies become your roadmap to realization.

Embrace this journey with open arms, for your dreams aren't just possible; they're just around the corner. The combination of a strong mindset and a well-crafted financial plan can propel you to heights you've never imagined.

The means of exchange is a fascinating theater of life, dreams, and success. It goes beyond money and delves into the core of what we desire and how we achieve it.

The road to RADical success starts with understanding the means of exchange, planning, visualizing, and executing. Your dreams are not only attainable; they are a reality waiting to happen.

Join us at RAD Strategic Partners as we take center stage in the theater of dreams and success. Together, we can create the pathway to realizing all that you desire. As your partner for RADical success, we're here for you every step of the way.

Action Item: Scripting Your Dream Pathway

1. **Dream Price Tag Calculation:** Set aside time this week for a dream session. Here, list your aspirations, no matter how big or small. Then, put a price tag on each.

2. **Revenue Roadmap:** Sketch out a revenue projection for the next five years. Include potential growth areas and diversification.

3. **Gap Analysis Act:** Now, step into the spotlight of the details. Where are you currently versus where do you want to be? Identify the gaps.

4. **Visualization Rehearsal:** Each morning, spend a few minutes visualizing your success.

5. **Action Steps Stage Direction:** Break down your dream into actionable steps. Start small, but be consistent.

6. **Belief Tune-Up:** Reflect on your self-beliefs and attitudes towards success and money. Are there any limiting beliefs holding you back?

7. **Feedback Encore:** Regularly seek feedback on your progress. Use this feedback to refine your steps and strategy.

8. **Plan Pivot Performance:** Be ready to pivot or adjust your plan based on the feedback you receive and the progress you make.

9. **Celebration Finale:** Celebrate every small win along the way. Each step forward is a step closer to your dream. These celebrations are your victory bows.

Why are we doing this? The pathway to your dreams combines practical planning, steadfast belief, and a dash of daring. At RAD Strategic Partners, we believe in the power of dreams coupled with actionable strategies.

Month 12

WHEN LEMONS APPEAR

Resilience in the Face of Adversity: Triumphing through RADical Challenges

As we venture into the final section of our journey, we confront an inevitable aspect of the pursuit of success: dealing with setbacks, rejections, and failures. This section is about building bulletproof resilience that turns every "wrong" into a stepping stone toward your goals.

First, we discuss how to dismiss rejection. Rejection, while stinging, is not the end—it's feedback. We'll explore strategies to detach from the negative emotions of rejection and use it as a catalyst for growth and refinement.

Then, we turn our attention to transforming failures into lessons. Failure is an invaluable teacher, and we'll delve into how to mine these experiences for insights that inform and improve your future endeavors.

Finding opportunities in threats is next. In every crisis lies the seed of opportunity. We'll learn to adopt a mindset that looks beyond immediate threats, identifying hidden possibilities for innovation and progress.

Lastly, we tackle facing challenges head-on. Challenges are not road blocks but invitations to demonstrate our creativity, courage, and determination. We'll cover practical ways to confront and overcome challenges, ensuring they become testimonies to your resilience and resourcefulness.

As we close this book, remember that setbacks are not stop signs but benchmarks on your path to RADical success. Are you ready to turn every "wrong" into your next big "right"? Let's navigate these final lessons together.

Week 49

DISMISS REJECTION: EMBRACING OPPORTUNITIES BEYOND FEAR

Fear of rejection is a universal experience, often ingrained in us from childhood. It's a trepidation that can significantly impact our lives, holding us back from seizing opportunities and achieving our goals. Understanding this fear and overcoming it is crucial for personal and professional growth.

The Roots of Rejection Fear

Rejection fear stems from various life experiences. Childhood events like being the last picked for a team or facing criticism during a class presentation plant the seeds of this fear. This fear is not just a personal sentiment; it's a collective experience shared by many.

The Mask of Avoidance

Often, we disguise our fear of rejection with excuses:

- "I'll get back to them tomorrow."
- "My business thrives on referrals only."
- "Networking or cold calling is a waste of time."
- "They are too important to take my call."

These excuses are a form of self-rejection, where we close the door to possibilities before even trying.

The Cost of Fear

The repercussions of letting fear control us are significant. We miss out on opportunities, lower our self-esteem, and limit our potential. Rejection is rarely about us as individuals; it's more about a mismatch of needs and timing.

Strategies to Overcome Rejection Fear

1. **Redefine the Narrative:** Change the story in your head. Understand that a "no" isn't a personal attack but perhaps a matter of bad timing or mismatched needs.
2. **Emulate the Tenacity of Children:** Children often show admirable persistence in asking for what they want, undeterred by rejection. Embracing this attitude can be transformative.
3. **Evaluate What's Lost:** Remember, if you didn't have it before asking, you haven't lost anything. It's crucial to differentiate between actual loss and the disappointment of unmet expectations.

Embracing Wayne Gretzky's Wisdom

Hockey legend Wayne Gretzky famously said, "You miss 100% of the shots you don't take." This quote highlights the importance of action over inaction. The fear of rejection should not prevent us from attempting and taking chances.

The Power of Positive Results

Confronting rejection fear involves facing it head-on and taking action despite the fear. Celebrate every small victory and positive result, as these are powerful tools for overcoming fear.

Rejection is integral to life and should not deter us from pursuing our dreams. By understanding and overcoming this fear, we open ourselves to a world of possibilities and take steps closer to RADical success.

> **"**
> You miss 100%
> of the shots you
> don't take.
> **"**

-Wayne Gretsky

Action Item: Rejection Reflection and Transformation

1. **Reflect on a Recent Rejection:** Think about a recent instance where you experienced rejection. It could be a denied proposal, an unreturned call, a missed job opportunity, or any other situation where you felt rejected.

2. **Document the Experience:** Write down the specific rejection scenario. Detail the context, your feelings, and the immediate outcome. This step is crucial for acknowledging and preparing to learn from the event.

3. **Analyze and Learn:** Next to the described rejection, jot down what you learned from this experience.

4. **Set a Proactive Goal:** Based on the insights gained, set a tangible goal for the upcoming month. This goal should be directed towards improving how you handle similar situations in the future.

5. **Embrace the Growth Mindset:** Understanding your reaction to rejection and transforming it into actionable goals is not just about recovery—it's about growth and resilience.

6. **Implement and Review:** Actively work towards your set goal. Midway through the month, review your progress.

This exercise is designed to help you shift your perspective on rejection. Instead of viewing it as a setback, see it as an opportunity for growth and learning. By transforming rejection into actionable insights, you're not just overcoming a hurdle but paving a path toward greater resilience and success.

Week 50

EMBRACE FAILURE: YOUR ROADMAP TO TURNING FAILURES INTO SUCCESS

The Dark Cloud of Failure

Failure is a term that can make even the most confident among us wince. It seems like the specter of failure looms everywhere. Businesses? A whopping 45% close shop within the first five years. Academics? Only 33% of public college students don the cap and gown in four years. The statistics paint a grim picture, but here at RAD Strategic Partners, we don't see failure as a full stop—it's a semicolon in the complex sentence of your journey toward success.

The "RADical Doctrine": Seeking Success, Not Failure

At RAD, we hold a family saying close to heart: "The best spots are at the end of dirt roads." But guess what? Some of those roads lead to a dead end. Now, don't turn around just yet; sometimes, the detour holds the real adventure. This principle is pivotal in understanding that failure isn't fatal; it's just a bump on the road. The average millionaire has faced bankruptcy 3.5 times. They don't see these as failures but as the cost of tuition in the university of success.

Four Steps to Move Through Fear and Toward Your Goals

1. **Shift Your Perspective on Failure**
   Reframe failure not as a personal flaw but as valuable data. Each failure gives insight into what didn't work, allowing you to course-correct. Fear often paralyzes us because we view failure as something catastrophic. If you can shift your mindset to see failure as a learning opportunity, fear loses much of its power. The sooner you see failure as feedback, the quicker you move forward.

2. **Take Incremental Action**
   Fear of failure often stems from thinking too far ahead. Break your goals down into smaller, manageable steps. Instead of the daunting big picture, focus on the next step. Taking small, calculated risks builds momentum and each small success you achieve chips away at the fear. Progress, no matter how small, helps you build confidence in overcoming challenges.

3. **Visualize the Worst-Case Scenario—and Your Response**
   Sometimes, the fear of failure is more overwhelming than the actual consequences. Take a moment to imagine the worst-case scenario if you fail. What would happen? How would you recover? Chances are, even in the worst-case scenario, you'll find ways to bounce back. By mentally preparing for what could go wrong, you build a sense of resilience, knowing that you can handle failure.

4. **Build a Support Network**
   Don't face the fear of failure alone. Surround yourself with mentors, peers, or a coach who can guide you through difficult times and provide constructive feedback. Often, the people in our support network help us see a failure from a different perspective, offering advice or encouragement when we need it most. Sharing your fears with others takes away its power and opens the door to solutions you might not have considered on your own.

The Psychology of Failure: A Deeper Dive

Studies have shown that failure affects our personal lives and mental makeup. It can induce a fear that inhibits our decision-making abilities. And this fear? It's contagious, passing down generations and affecting the quality of our lives and businesses. This is where RAD's coaching comes into play. We help you break the cycle by focusing on long-term visions rather than short-term setbacks.

Learning from Legends

Historical figures like Winston Churchill, who said, "Success always demands a greater effort," have shared wisdom that echoes through time. They were no strangers to failure but used it as fuel to achieve monumental success. Their stories aren't just stories; they are lessons woven into the fabric of success.

A RADical Perspective on Failure

When you aim for the stars, failure becomes a mere obstacle rather than an endpoint. A wrong turn isn't a tragedy; it's a chance to discover something new. So, put failure in the rearview mirror and press the gas pedal on your road to RADical success.

RADical Moves: Your Action Step for Success

You're charged up and ready to turn those so-called failures into stepping stones. But what's the immediate next step? Simple.

Action Item: Write down one "failure" you've experienced in the past six months. Next to it, jot down at least one lesson you learned from it. Now, translate that lesson into a proactive goal for the next month.

Why are we doing this? As we say at RAD Strategic Partners, understanding failure is the first step toward converting it into fuel for your RADical success journey. By identifying your lessons and setting actionable goals, you're not just stopping at insights—you're translating them into a game plan.

Week 51

TURN THREATS INTO OPPORTUNITIES: TURNING CHALLENGES INTO GROWTH

Embracing Change Amidst Global Challenges

Many individuals and businesses face unpredictable challenges as we have experienced with the pandemic, fears of economic recession, wars, and unprecedented weather events. From layoffs to economic downturns, the threat is real and can seem overwhelming. However, it is crucial to remember that all risks are also opportunities. In fact, many hazards can bring about new opportunities and growth. In this chapter, we will explore how threats can bring opportunities and share some stories of opportunities created by threats.

Economic Impact and Job Market Shifts

One of the most significant threats that businesses and individuals face is the ongoing economic impact of the pandemic and the resulting changes in buying patterns and consumer behavior. Early in the COVID-19 pandemic, the International Labour Organization (ILO) predicted the pandemic would wipe out 6.7% of working hours globally in the second quarter of 2021.[34] This is

---

[34] ILO Monitor: COVID-19 and the world of work. 2nd Edition (https://www.ilo.org/resource/brief/ilo-monitor-covid-19-and-world-work-2nd-edition)

equivalent to 195 million full-time workers losing their jobs. Yet, that didn't happen. Instead, the USA experienced consistent record job growth, and the labor force participation rates reached record highs[35] Many people lost jobs, but many new opportunities were created, frequently leading to higher pay and job satisfaction.

Digital Transformation as a Strategic Advantage

One of the ways that businesses can turn threats into opportunities is by embracing digital transformation. As a result of recent events, many companies adopted new technologies to facilitate remote work and online commerce. Companies that had already invested in digital transformation were better equipped to weather the pandemic. They could quickly adapt to changing market conditions and maintain business continuity. In fact, a study by the European Investment Bank found that companies that invested in digital transformation before the pandemic were twice as likely to report increased revenue and profits during the crisis.[36]

The Rise of E-Commerce

Another opportunity that has emerged is the growth of e-commerce. With more people staying at home, there has been a surge in online shopping. Global e-commerce sales reached $5.7 trillion in 2022, up from $3.5 trillion in 2019. This change presents a significant opportunity for businesses to expand their online presence and reach new customers.

---

[35] https://www.bls.gov/opub/ted/2023/labor-force-participation-rate-for-people-ages-25-to-54-in-may-2023-highest-since-january-2007.htm
[36] https://www.eib.org/en/press/all/2022-214-the-2021-2022-digitalisation-in-europe-report-the-pandemic-has-made-the-digital-transformation-an-integral-part-of-european-society

Personal Development and Community Engagement

However, opportunities are not limited to the business world. Individuals can also turn threats into opportunities by embracing new hobbies and skills. For example, with more time at home, many people have taken up cooking, gardening, or fitness. According to research published in Frontiers in Psychology, 68% of respondents said they had tried a new hobby or activity during the pandemic. [37] Doing so not only provides a distraction from the stresses of daily life but can also lead to personal growth and self-improvement.

Leveraging Technology for Social Connection

In addition to personal growth, recent events highlighted the importance of community and social connection. While physical distancing measures forced people to stay apart, they also spurred creativity and innovation. For example, many people have turned to virtual platforms to stay connected with friends and family. According to a survey by GlobalWebIndex, the use of video conferencing apps such as Zoom and Skype increased by 70% in the first half of 2020.[38] This technology presents an opportunity for individuals to connect with people they may not be able to see in person.

Seizing Opportunities for Innovation

In conclusion, while life presents significant challenges for individuals and businesses, it is important to remember that all risks are opportunities. By embracing digital transformation, expanding their online presence, developing new skills and hobbies, staying connected with others, and prioritizing mental health and well-being, individuals and businesses can turn threats into opportunities for growth and innovation.

---

[37] Morse, K. F., Fine, P. A., & Friedlander, K. J., "Creativity and Leisure During COVID-19: Examining the Relationship Between Leisure Activities, Motivations, and Psychological Well-Being," *Frontiers in Psychology, 12*. (2021) https://doi.org/10.3389/fpsyg.2021.609967
[38] https://www.gwi.com/reports/trends-2020

Action Steps: Harnessing Opportunities from Threats

This week, take the time to turn perceived threats into actionable opportunities. Here's how you can start:

1. **Identify a Threat:** Choose a recent threat or challenge in your personal life or business. It could be something as small as a new competitor in your market or as significant as adapting to remote work.
2. **Assess the Opportunity:** Write down how this threat could be seen as an opportunity. For instance, could a competitor push you to innovate? Does remote work offer a chance to explore digital transformation?
3. **Create a Plan:** Develop a small, actionable plan to capitalize on this opportunity. This could involve researching new technologies, brainstorming with your team, or taking a course to develop a new skill.
4. **Implement and Reflect:** Put your plan into action and observe the results. At the end of the week, reflect on the changes you've made and the lessons learned. Did the threat turn into an opportunity? How has this shift in perspective impacted your approach to challenges?
5. **Share Your Experience:** Write down your insights and share them with your team or peers. Discuss how viewing threats as opportunities can lead to growth and innovation.

Why are we doing this? At RAD Strategic Partners, we understand that every threat hides a potential opportunity. By shifting our mindset to view challenges as stepping stones, we can open doors to unexpected growth and success. This exercise is designed to turn theory into practice, fostering a proactive approach to overcoming obstacles.

Embrace the challenge, and let's turn threats into thriving opportunities for RADical success!

Week 52

FACE CHALLENGES HEAD-ON: NAVIGATING THE BUSINESS JUNGLE WITH A SMILE

Today, we're diving headfirst into the wild and wonderful world of facing challenges. In this chapter, we'll explore why confronting challenges head-on is essential for success, learn how to develop a resilient mindset, and include some case studies and statistics to back it up.

Embrace the Challenge with a Smile

Imagine yourself as a fearless explorer in the heart of the business jungle. When challenges arise, don't let them bring you down. Instead, meet them with a smile. Think of challenges as opportunities in disguise—chances to grow, learn, and discover new paths to success.

Remember, a smile is your secret weapon. It disarms the challenge, giving you the confidence to confront it head-on. So, put on your best "challenge accepted" grin, and let's get started!

Shift Your Mindset: From Obstacle to Opportunity

To face challenges head-on, you need to cultivate a resilient mindset. Start by reframing your perception of obstacles. Instead of seeing them as roadblocks, view them as stepping stones toward your goals. Challenges are your chance to showcase your problem-solving skills and resilience.

Think of challenges as puzzles waiting to be solved. Embrace the thrill of finding creative solutions and uncovering hidden opportunities. Adopting this mindset makes even the most daunting challenges become exciting adventures.

The Domino's Pizza turnaround is an excellent example of this. In the late 2000s, Domino's received widespread criticism for the quality of their pizza. Rather than ignoring or dismissing the feedback, Domino's took it as an opportunity to revamp its entire brand and product.

They launched an advertising campaign to acknowledge their mistakes and promised to improve. Domino's invested heavily in improving its recipes, ingredients, and delivery service. Domino's successfully turned its business around by confronting the challenge directly and implementing changes based on customer feedback. Today, they are the largest pizza chain in the world based on revenue and the world's fifth-largest quick-serve restaurant.[39]

Analyze, Strategize, Execute

Once you've adjusted your mindset, it's time to dive into the nitty-gritty of tackling challenges. A systematic approach is crucial for success.

---

[39] https://www.pmq.com/dominos-now-the-largest-pizza-chain-in-the-world/

1. **Analyze the Challenge:** Break it down into smaller, manageable parts. Identify the root causes, potential risks, and available resources. This analysis will help you gain clarity and understand the landscape you're navigating.
2. **Strategize Your Plan of Attack:** Consider various solutions, weigh their pros and cons, and choose the one that aligns with your goals and resources. Creativity often thrives in constraint, so think outside the box and explore innovative approaches.
3. **Execute Your Plan:** Take action with determination and tenacity. Be prepared for twists and turns, but don't let them deter you. Adapt and adjust your approach as needed, keeping your eyes firmly on the prize.

Seek Support from Fellow Explorers

No explorer ventures into the unknown alone. In the business jungle, seeking support from fellow adventurers is vital. Connect with mentors, coaches, or like-minded individuals who can offer guidance, insights, and encouragement.

Sharing your challenges with others can provide fresh perspectives and alternative solutions. Remember, laughter is often the best medicine in tough times, so find fellow explorers who can add a touch of humor to your journey.

Learn from Failure and Celebrate Success

Challenges come with ups and downs. Celebrate your successes, no matter how small, and use them as fuel to keep going. At the same time, don't fear failure. Embrace it as a valuable teacher that provides essential lessons for growth.

Take a moment to reflect on your experiences, both triumphs and setbacks. What worked? What didn't? Learn from your failures, adjust your approach, and keep moving forward. Remember, the accurate measure of success lies not in avoiding challenges but in how you overcome them.

The Small Business Administration reports that over 50% of small businesses fail within the first five years. Those who survive often credit their success to their ability to tackle challenges head-on, adapt to market conditions, and innovate in the face of adversity.

Remember, challenges are not roadblocks but stepping stones to greatness. Embrace them with humor, analyze them precisely, and execute your plans confidently. Seek support from fellow adventurers and celebrate every step forward.

So, go forth with a grin on your face, knowing that you have the power to conquer any challenge that comes your way.

Remember, the life and business jungle awaits, and it's time to show it who's boss!

Final Action Steps: Embracing Challenges with a Smile

As we conclude our journey through this book, let's embrace our final challenge with optimism and determination. This week, focus on facing life's hurdles head-on, navigating each day's jungle with a resilient smile.

1. **Reflect on Your Journey:** Take a moment to reflect on the challenges you've faced over the past year. Write down the significant hurdles and how you approached them. Acknowledge both your successes and the lessons learned from less successful attempts.
2. **Identify a Current Challenge:** Choose a challenge in your life or business. It could be a personal goal, a professional project, or a situation that requires a strategic approach.
3. **Develop a Positive Plan:** Craft a plan to tackle this challenge, focusing on maintaining a positive attitude throughout. Incorporate strategies from previous chapters that have resonated with you the most.
4. **Implement with Optimism:** As you put your plan into action, consciously maintain a positive mindset. Remember, your attitude can significantly influence outcomes. Even in moments of doubt, keep a smile and look for the silver lining.
5. **Celebrate and Share:** At the end of the week, celebrate your progress, no matter how small. Share your experience with someone—a friend, a colleague, or a family member. Discuss how facing challenges with a positive attitude has impacted your approach to life and business.

CONCLUSION:
YOUR RADICAL JOURNEY AWAITS

As we bring our journey through *RADical Success Every Week: 52 Breakthrough Strategies for Business and Life* to a close, remember that this isn't the end—it's a vibrant new beginning. Over these twelve sections and fifty-two chapters, you've been equipped with actionable insights, strategies, and the empowering mindset necessary to forge your path to success.

Each chapter, with its unique action item, has been designed to inspire and provoke real change and progress. Whether you've followed along week by week or dipped in and out as needed, know that the journey toward RADical success is uniquely yours. It's about taking what resonates, applying it, and continuously evolving.

But the journey doesn't have to end here. If you've found value in these pages and are craving more, there are myriad ways we can keep this momentum alive together.

- **Expand Your Journey:** For those who wish to delve deeper, an online course based on the principles of this book awaits. It's a space to explore these concepts further, implement them, and see tangible results.
- **Get Personalized Guidance:** If one-to-one coaching speaks to your needs, I am here to partner with you. Together, we can tailor these principles to fit your unique circumstances, challenges, and aspirations.

- **Connect and Collaborate:** I am also available for speaking events and workshops. These gatherings are wonderful opportunities to connect, share experiences, and grow together in a dynamic, interactive environment.

Your engagement doesn't have to be a leap; it can be a simple step toward greater understanding, support, and success. The resources and recommendations within these chapters, accessible on the RAD Strategic Partners website, are also there to guide you further.

Remember, RADical success isn't a destination; it's a continuous, exhilarating journey. Every step, every decision, and every challenge faced head-on is part of crafting a life and business that's not just successful but meaningful and fulfilling.

Thank you for embarking on this journey with me. Here's to your continued growth, transformation, and RADical success. Let's keep moving forward together.

Angie

ABOUT THE AUTHOR

Angie Dobransky, Founder of RAD Strategic Partners

Angie is a seasoned business coach with a wealth of expertise and a flair for infusing subtle humor into her work. As the founder of RAD Strategic Partners, she has dedicated her career to helping individuals and organizations achieve RADical success. With a deep understanding of leadership, success, mindset, and business dynamics, Angie has become a sought-after mentor for those striving to reach their full potential.

Based in the vibrant DC metro area, Angie brings a unique blend of experience and creativity to her coaching. Not only is she a seasoned professional in the business world, but she also considers herself a true Renaissance woman. Her passion for creating things—be it jewelry, papercrafts, or other crafts—adds a personal touch to her professional endeavors.

Angie's approach to coaching is rooted in love and kindness, always aiming to help people become their best selves. Her insightful guidance and inclusive perspective make her an inspiring figure in the business community. Angie focuses on fostering an environment where everyone can thrive.

When she's not coaching or crafting, Angie often engages in deep conversations about business and personal success, topics she can discuss for hours. Her ability to connect with others and drive positive change is evident in her work and the lives of those she mentors.

Angie is now sharing her wealth of knowledge and experience in her new book, providing readers with the tools and insights they need to navigate their paths to success. Join her on this journey and discover the RADical potential within you.

Connect with Angie

Web: @www.radstrategic.com
LinkedIn: @yourpartnerforsuccess
Facebook: @CoachAngieDobransky
Twitter: @angiedobransky
Instagram: @radstrategicpartners
YouTube: @radstrategicpartners

ALSO BY THE AUTHOR

Life Lessons in Success: Wisdom to Win the Game of Life

Angie's first book, *Life Lessons in Success: Wisdom to Win the Game of Life*, is available on Amazon and wherever books are sold. In this inspiring work, Angie and thirty-five of her friends share personal stories and the lessons they learned to help readers navigate the complexities of life and achieve personal and professional success.

Let's Keep the Momentum Going!

You've taken the steps to explore RADical Success, now let's take things even further together. Whether you want to dive deeper into the resources mentioned in this book or explore how we can work together to achieve your goals, I'm here to help!

Access Bonus Content and Book Resources

Scan this code to unlock all the tools, worksheets, and bonus content referenced throughout the book. Everything you need to take action and achieve RADical success!

Connect with Angie Dobransky

Ready to take your business or personal success to the next level? Scan here to connect with me directly! Let's explore how we can work together to make your goals a reality.

Let's continue your RADical journey together. Whether you're looking for personalized coaching, speaking engagements, or strategic business guidance, I'm here to be your partner in success.

Visit me at: www.radstrategic.com